W9-ADL-575

In Rooms
of Memory

AMERICAN LIVES

Series editor

Tobias Wolff

In Rooms
of Memory

Essays

HILARY MASTERS

University of Nebraska Press

Lincoln and London

Library of Congress
Cataloging-in-Publication Data

Masters, Hilary.
In rooms of memory : essays /
Hilary Masters.
p.   cm. — (American lives)
ISBN 978-0-8032-2271-7
(cloth : alk. paper)
I. Title.
PS3563.A821525   2009
814'.54—dc22
2009006658

Set in Adobe Garamond Pro
by Bob Reitz.
Designed by A. Shahan.

For Kathleen

Contents

Acknowledgments

Several of the essays in this volume were originally published elsewhere: "Chimera," "Passing through Pittsburgh," and "Unwired" in *Creative NonFiction*; "Disorderly Conduct" in the *New England Review*; "My Father's Image" in *New Letters;* "In My Orchard" in the *North American Review*; "Making It Up" and "In Montaigne's Tower" in the *Ohio Review*; "In Rooms of Memory" and "In the Cards" in *Prairie Schooner*; and "Double Exposure," "The End of Something," "Going to Cuba," and "Proud Flesh" in the *Sewanee Review*.

"In My Orchard" and "In Rooms of Memory" were named Notable Essays of 2005 and 2006, respectively, by Robert Atwan in *Best American Essays*. "Going to Cuba" received the Monroe Spears Award from the *Sewanee Review*. Phillip Lopate chose "In Montaigne's Tower" as one of the *Anchor Best Essays of 1998*. "Making It Up" was included by Edward Hoagland in *Best American Essays of 1999*.

The author expresses his profound gratitude to these editors and journals for their encouragement.

In Rooms
of Memory

Going to Cuba

A sketch by Chekhov recounts the incident of two rural constables escorting an old vagrant to the local workhouse. The day is hot and their journey has been long and dusty. They decide to rest a little by the side of the road. The old man has refused to tell them his name or where he is from, but as he relaxes on the ground, he begins to spin a fancy of his homeland—a place of wondrous plenty: clear, cool streams from which fish leap to catch themselves on lines; berries and fruits fall ripe into outstretched hands; milk and honey and always fair weather. His description enthralls the other two; they are carried away by his fantasy. Then one of them snaps out of it, and they get back on the road. But, for a moment, both prisoner and police have been set free.

Our imaginations, often falsely confirmed by memory, can cross many borders, but these escapes are doomed and freedom always lies just beyond. For example, if I were to go out my door here on Monterey Street in Pittsburgh, take a right at the YMCA on the corner, then continue in a southeasterly direction across the point where the Allegheny and the Monongahela rivers agree to become the Ohio, and then, if I were still to continue this same range athwart the southern states, my next landfall would be Cuba. Just beyond Cuba lies the Isle of Pines.

"Where is the Isle of Pines?" It is August of 1951, and the basement dive of Louis's on Sheridan Square is a frosty enclave within the steamed province of Greenwich Village. Rosemary Clooney is singing "C'mon to My House," and the woman who has just sat down at my table has jumped up to dance to the quasi-Arabic melody, swaying in her summer dress to the blast of the jukebox. No one takes any notice of her; she moves within a cell of her own, a figurine turning within a bell jar.

Someone is always playing the song, always feeding the jukebox so that Clooney sings without let-up until closing time, which it is close to right now. Three a.m. Just before, while Clooney takes a break, this blonde walks over from the bar and sits down at my table. She doesn't seem to be with anyone, and she carries a worn leather portfolio under one arm. Out of this folder she has taken a newspaper clipping and hands it to me. She is very pale with stringy hair and eyes of beer-bottle green that seem to slide off into the whites around the pupils.

"C'mon to my house, c'mon to my house . . . c'mon," Clooney starts up again. "I give you ca-nn-dy."

This woman has just asked me to go to Cuba with her, to the Isle of Pines, then jumps up to dance by herself, not waiting for my answer nor hearing my question. Her bare feet pivot and shuffle on the sawdusted floor of the bar, and she gives herself to the music in a way that seems to be a demonstration of something. I think of the women in Robinson Jeffers's poetry. Wild. Primitive. Probably dangerous.

So when she sits down, I have to ask her again. She is a little breathless and tastes a droplet of moisture above her lips before she answers.

"It's an island off the south coast of Cuba," she tells me. "I own one hundred acres on the beach. They've discovered oil on my property. What do you think?" She motioned to the newspaper clipping in my hand. "Will he die?"

The picture that goes with the article shows the mangled wreckage of a Jaguar convertible smashed against a large tree in Cleveland or Columbus. The horrific hybrid has produced a senseless being who, the account says, lies in a coma, near death in a hospital. His injuries are severe and numerous. "Do you think he'll die?" she asks once more.

"Doesn't look good," I say. Her expression is distant, a gaze for a moor or some desolate tundra, and I see not a shadow of concern or anxiety. Only a cool calculation. "Do you know him?"

"He's my husband," she says. "As soon as the son of a bitch dies, I'm going to Cuba. Why don't you come with me? The Isle of Pines."

Going to Cuba. In the smoky, mechanically frigid zone of Louis's, the tropical island rises in my imagination like a great ship, safely anchored in an artery waiting for the flood tide. The smell of disinfectant from the men's room becomes the aroma of conifers. I can see the surf curling around the beach like a cuff of lace.

This summer I have been attending lectures in Anglo-Saxon and Old English at Columbia to make up for courses I slept through during the previous year at my home university. My GI Bill is about to run out, but I am not all that interested in finishing my degree, at least not at my university, which has become a preppy, hostile stockade around my dreams of becoming a writer. Some of my contemporaries were already living in the Village and chatting up the resident literati at places like Chumley's or the White Horse. I wasn't even living in the Village, and my time in New York was given to making up failed courses. Other contemporaries have already jumped into the currents of their careers as copyboys at the *Times* or UPI or into lower echelon jobs in publishing, freelancing reviews in magazines.

I don't want a career; I want experience. I want to write—and

3

didn't Hemingway say that to become a writer, experience had to be gained? And where was he getting his experience then? Cuba.

Moreover, Delmore Schwartz and Dwight McDonald are not my mentors, as they are for others. My current master is the old poet Maxwell Bodenheim, whose watery-eyed perception of my apprenticeship, as I would sit across from him at the San Remo, tested no more of my potential than the next cheap Chianti. What would Max think of this offer? I ask myself. Would he pick up and go to the Isle of Pines with this strange woman?

—Where is the Isle of Pines?

—Off the coast of Cuba, Max. Should I go there to write?

—Hell, yes, go there. These Chicago winters are going to kill me one day.

But of course we are in New York, so Bodenheim is wrong on both counts, and I give serious consideration to this willowy blonde's offer. It is nearly three a.m. at Louis's in Greenwich Village on Sheridan Square in 1951. Dancing in her bare feet, self absorbed and strangely calm, I decide to call her Tamar. Red, the bartender, whose hair is actually on the silvery side, begins to ease people over their final beers.

"Well, he's still alive," Tamar reports. She's just returned from the pay phone at the back, after taking all the change I had. A small enough investment, I have reasoned.

"You called the hospital?" Was it Akron or Toledo?

"He's still in a coma. Pelvis smashed. What's the thorax?"

"Chest." Red has caught my eye and looks meaningfully at the stairs that lead up to the street.

"That too," she says. The Jaguar had been traveling at a terrific rate of speed and the driver had been very drunk.

The summer's anthem starts up once more and Clooney la-de-dahs Saroyan's lyrics as if they were an epilogue for the evening.

4

Cleverly, I make a deft transition. "C'mon to my house—c'mon," I croon to this pallid creature with eyes that seem to have no back to them. As we climb the steps into the humid heaviness of the August night, I am thinking that no troubadour could have done better with his Auvergne shepherdess.

This summer I am driving a 1946 Ford Anglia that looks like a normal car from the side but, on turning a corner, the vehicle nearly becomes a vertical line, like a car in a cartoon. Also, the floorboards on the passenger side are sketchy, and my passenger's skirt billows in the updraft like a spinnaker as she holds her cracked sandals in her lap. We putt-putt up Seventh Avenue, still a two-way thoroughfare then, and Tamar hugs her briefcase and seems to enjoy the ride.

Yet, I expect her to have me stop at any moment as we journey north, and I run a couple of lights so as not to give her the chance to change her mind. There's a cool madness about her that suggests her natural habitat lies below Fourteenth Street, and I wonder if transporting her into the rarefied atmosphere of the Upper West Side might wring a mortal change in her. I glance at her face. Her features remain composed in their fixed serenity: no sudden wrinkling around the eyes, no catastrophic hollowing of the cheeks.

"Who is this Tamar you keep calling me?" she asks when we join Broadway at Thirty-fourth.

Indeed, I have renamed her—a preliminary to possession that at least one of us recognizes—though my nomination has dubious authority because of my confusion of Jeffers's heroines. I've mixed up the murderous, hot-blooded Tamar with the barefoot loving shepherdess who gives up her life defending her lambs, a confusion I am to have with more than one woman.

As we go up Broadway I give her a quick gloss of Jeffers's poetry, at least my study of it in my father's library a few years back, where the falling line accounts of lust between brother and sister, woman and woman, and even—I leave this out—woman and stallion often inspired a sexual frenzy in me not experienced since reading Zola and Maupassant.

"There's a phone booth," she says suddenly. We are passing through the intersection of Fifty-seventh Street, Columbus Circle just ahead. The doings at Point Sur have held no interest for her.

"You just called the hospital, just before we left Louis's," I say and keep my foot down on the gas pedal. The Anglia's four cylinders are generating a lot of heat, and sweat is popping out on my brow, trickling down from my armpits. The little car has become a portable oven. But Tamar looks cool and comfortable, though I wonder how she will fare in my room on 104th Street. One window on the building's airshaft, one small sink in the corner, and one chair. The stale sheets on the narrow bed, where only this afternoon I listlessly studied the conjugation of *lufian*, a traditional paradigm of a weak verb and meaning "to love."

"Maybe he's had a sinking spell," Tamar reasons.

"I don't have any more silver," I say.

"We can get change," she says.

"Where? It's after three in the morning!"

"In a subway. They make change all night in the subway."

I press on. The Anglia is making all the sequential green lights on Central Park West, all in one run. On our right the park looks inviting, a more natural and attractive alternative to my close and sultry room, but I'm afraid her Jeffers persona might take over. I can imagine her running off, barefoot, into the urban woods around the Reservoir to emerge on the East Side—gone forever.

Even when I park across from my building, I still expect her to flee downtown, but she follows me almost meekly across the street and waits, shoes in hand, as I unlock the apartment's main door. As we rise in the elevator I am thinking that I am about to *lufian* a woman who is almost a widow, that to lie between her thighs I will replace a man who lies horribly mangled and near death because of a passion that had driven him into a sycamore tree. The elevator labors to altitude and my heart spins like a turbocharger. That Tamar travels light and has no place to sleep has not occurred to me.

But this summer of 1951, I am borrowing more than books from my father's library and the urgencies of mind and matter they inspire. His history has also become a study for me, a curiosa to browse. He has just died the year before, and this final abandonment has led me to trace his and my mother's path around New York, to follow the outline of their lives, lived without me, before it becomes grown over in memory. Like a child who puts on a parent's clothes to gain intimacy, I have been putting on the accoutrements of my parents' history so that I might come to know them better. It is, of course, a charade and, like all "dress-up" games, made silly by daylight.

Until I was fourteen, my maternal grandparents cared for me in Kansas City, Missouri. My mother left me with them when I was able to make the transfer from breast to bottle, at a year old, and returned to New York to be with my father. Their reasons for this arrangement I have put down elsewhere, but they still mystify me.

However, she would return for brief visits, sometimes to take me back to New York for a week or two with my father, and then she would return me to my grandmother's house on Roberts Street. Her entrances into that small house were always noisy and exciting, as if the Barnum and Bailey circus parade had turned off of Independence Avenue to come down our street. She spoke of restaurants they had eaten at, important writers and artists they had met, of the artists' studios visited in Greenwich Village. She was like the press agent for a calamitous, triumphant road show, though I am to learn later that these outlandish advertisements of their life were mostly fabricated to convince her parents the marriage was okay, that all was well, and to court the stern opinion of her father by this show of success.

To listen to her, my parents seemed to own Greenwich Village and much of the rest of Manhattan. In Kansas City I became acquainted with the Jumble Shop on the corner of McDougal and Eighth Street. I could visualize the lobbies of the Brevort and the Lafayette hotels and the funny things that went on there. I heard about exotic places like Romany Marie's and a German restaurant that sounded Chinese—Luchow's. In 1951 Greenwich Village has not changed so much from their day, but I know little more about their passage through it. I cannot afford to enter Charles French Restaurant, where my father was supposed to favor the crepes, nor can I find Romany Marie's. Edna Millay's little house, she has just died also, is just as my mother described it and so is the Greenwich Mews, where Mae Mott Smith had her studio. The inner courtyard of Patchin Place looks the same through the iron grill gate, though I'm not sure of the unit where the Welsh novelist John Cowper Powys served them tea by a cozy fireplace.

"e.e. cummings lives there now," I tell Tamar. This is later in the week, and that afternoon we have just made reservations to fly to Havana. She is impatient to take flight—probably impatient with my guided tour as well. She looks around Sixth Avenue for a phone booth. So even as she calls Akron or Toledo, I am trying to put on parts of my parents' life, none of which fit me even if I could afford the garb.

The little sum I have managed to save from my GI allowance is supplemented by the four bucks earned every weekday in a delicatessen in the garment district. This goes mostly for beers at Louis's or an occasional symposium with Bodenheim at the San Remo. Every day, starting at eleven o'clock after my classes at Columbia, I take orders over the phone for sandwiches and bagels, custards and Jell-O puddings that are then delivered by a couple of black kids to nearby offices. These guys, like me, also get their lunch, and, at the end of our stint, the three of us are given brown-bag bonuses of bagels and containers of cream cheese and potato salad. Sometimes a little lox or a piece of brisket. These provisions usually do me for supper.

But I envy the delivery boys for they get something extra. Their lunchtime missions take them into the frenetic environs where women's clothing is being designed and fabricated, where the silken confinements of women's bodies were being fitted in place at such a fever pitch that the very sandwiches delivered probably lay half eaten at the end of the day.

"Where are you going?" Tamar's voice is muffled this first morning; her face is pressed into the one pillow on the bed. The shade drawn down to the windowsill flaps idly in a humid breeze to play a brilliant scarf of light upon her naked rump. "We're just getting to sleep."

I am painfully aware of this fact as I slowly pull on my clothes. "I have to go to work," I tell her. My body is sore, blood has been drawn. She is everything Robinson Jeffers claimed she would be.

I tell her about my job, that I'll be back in a few hours and she should get some sleep. Delicacy keeps me from mentioning that I had missed my eight o'clock class in Old English. The small gash just below my rib cage—Tamar's nails were long and crimson—had happened just as everyone else was discussing the position of the negative *ne* before the verb, a convention that was to disappear with Middle English. That had been part of the day's assignment.

Tamar has slipped into a deep sleep.

My response to the ringing telephone at the delicatessen is Pavlovian perfect. As I take down orders for cheese and ham sandwiches,

I review the other hot work that has only recently employed me. Tamar enclosed our lust within narratives, her feathery voice recounting details of her married life, and this running account inspired reenactments of that history. More than once in the hours before dawn, she had risen from the swampy mire of my narrow bed to talk about her husband, the man whose death we waited on. She had shivered, the chill of her own cooling sweat upon her, as she told me the things he had done to her. Her jolly breasts trembled like the noses of lambs.

"He would take me downtown to the finest stores," she told me. "Take me and buy me wonderful clothes. Go with me into the fitting rooms as I tried everything on. Everything. And everything was expensive. Underwear of lace and silk. Nylon stockings. Slips. Then dresses, blouses. Everything. He'd buy all these things. Then, at home, he has me go into the bedroom and put everything on, and then he would come into the bedroom. He would rip all these new, beautiful clothes off of me. Tear them off. Everything. Sometimes he would use scissors and cut them off. Everything. Cut them to ribbons. If I were wearing a blouse, he would take both his hands and rip it apart so the buttons would pop off on the floor. Pop-pop-pop." She demonstrated the attack, pulling her fists away from her chest suddenly and her breasts looked even more naked in the dim light. She panted as if she had just crossed the finish line of a race.

"No kidding," I said. "Why did he do that?" The man's wastefulness appalled me.

She had no answer, none that she could articulate, for she frowned a little. Then the scrap of a smile curled her lips. "Sometimes, he would tie me to one of the bedposts. We had an antique four-poster with a lacy canopy above. And then . . ." a sudden fatigue slurred her voice and pulled at her eyelids.

"And then?" My bed was little more than a studio couch.

". . . Unspeakable things," Tamar whispered in my ear and pulled me down with her into the stew of another feverish reverie.

As always, I have used the subway this morning, leaving the Anglia parked across from my apartment. Sometimes I would leave the car there for days—this is 1951 after all. So, when I walk from the subway on Broadway and 103rd and round the corner of Central Park West, I find Tamar sitting on the front step of my building, holding her white sandals in one hand and shielding her eyes with the other to peer into the territory of Central Park across the way. She looks fragile and forlorn, bleached to a near transparency by the midday heat, and resembles one of those prairie women in a Walker Evans photograph. Instantly I know she had dressed and gone out of the building to phone Ohio and has not been able to get back in.

"He's developed pneumonia," she says as she rises to greet me. Her gaze looks hopefully at me for confirmation—this is a good sign?

"How about something to eat?" I hold up the bag of goodies from the deli.

We find some shade under a tree in the park, and I lay out the provisions on a flat piece of black shale, feeling very much the provider returned from the hunt. I have set down bagels, cream cheese, and pieces of pressed ham. My employers have also thrown in a couple of pretty ripe bananas. The day has become beastly hot. "We could use some *showres soote*," I say.

"Sure," Tamar nods and smiles. "But maybe we can get a Coke or something later." She is an oracle who knows the answer and isn't telling.

She picks at the ham and makes ladylike decisions, taking one piece rather than another, while holding the bagel in a unique style. She's stuck her index finger through the hole and nibbles around the edges as if to acknowledge the bagel's design, if not suggest the original mode of its consumption, perhaps just discovered in Ohio.

Sucking off the ham residue from her fingers, she uses this hand to open the soft leather portfolio that seems to be her only baggage. I see handkerchiefs and cosmetics, some underclothing, and folders of papers that have a valuable appearance. Perhaps there's a will among them. Some have borders printed in pale blue and brown like bonds. She has pulled out a different kind of document. Its many folds are worn thin, completely through in some places, and she carefully lays it out on the rock, taking small bites around the bagel. She has unfolded a survey map.

"Here is my property. See, here's the beach. The town of Nueva Gerona is just a few miles this way." She points off the map to where ants are busy in a crack in the rock. The printing is in Spanish. Lines cross and intersect. "The house is old, but we can live in it while we build a new one. Closer to the beach. You'll be able to hear the trade winds as you write. They will ruffle your hair and your papers."

"How do you come to own this place?"

"My mother left it to me. See, here is her name at the bottom. *Pro-pie-tario*. And they have discovered oil on the property."

"Yes, you told me. You've been there, you've seen it?"

Her yellow hair flags down my question for its triviality. "Of course not. How could I?" I have no answer for that. "Pan American flies to Havana," she continues. "We must make reservations. From Havana, we take the train, only an hour or two, to the port of Batabano. Then we take a small boat, probably a ferry, across the gulf. To my island."

Only then I admit to myself I have been going along with this story of hers—the Isle of Pines and the rest of it—not just to get her into my bed, but to tease this fantasy I have of a writer's life. One should be comfortable while entertaining the Muse, and, like most young writers, I thought the workplace was crucial to the work. Even one and the same. Warm weather, sandy beaches, and all the mangoes you can eat—that's where the real work is to be done. Look at Hemingway, I keep reminding myself! So, it is a scary moment for me when I realize that I believe her. Here in the tropical simmer of Central Park, this strange woman has laid out for me the deed to a fantasy. It's the genuine article. She does own part of a Caribbean Island. She does want to take me there. This worn and ravaged angel landed next to me at Louis's and offered me a dream, a comfortable shortcut to literary success.

Tamar has begun to fold up the map, her expression cheerful and eyes downcast. Her face is pink with the heat. She only uses one hand, demonstrating an expertise with the map's seams and double pleats, while she continues to take bites of bagel impaled on the other. She's nibbled it down to a small ring around her finger, which, with a demure glance, she slips deep into her mouth to pull off the last morsel.

By chance, my grandfather had sent me one of the several pension checks he receives every month for his different services as a young man, subduing natives on the western frontier and parts of Central America. As we share the better banana of our picnic, I think it would be nice to buy Tamar some new shoes and then take her to dinner someplace. An outlet store near the subway on Broadway has stacks of name-brand shoes marked down to very low prices. She will step ashore on the Isle of Pines in decent footwear at least. I could buy her a new dress also, but she might get the wrong idea.

She wears the stiff leather sandals with a quiet delight to dinner that night at Schiavi's, an Italian place in the west thirties near the main post office on Eighth Avenue. "My mother used to bring me here when I was on vacations from school. Christmastime mostly." Tamar helps herself to more soup from the tureen and says nothing. "Same place, same meal, but only a dollar in those days. The lady at the cash register with the dyed red hair is Mrs. Schiavi. She looks the same too."

I am to learn that these dinners, cheap as they were, always put my mother in hock for a little. She and my father had separated by then, and she had just been hired to teach composition and literature at the Bentley School on West Eighty-sixth Street. Her salary was one thousand dollars a year. So, every time I arrived at the Greyhound Terminal on Thirty-fourth Street, only a couple of blocks from where Tamar and I are sipping the minestrone, my mother would have already visited a pawn shop, putting up the silver pepper grinder and the paired salt dish to raise a few bucks to stake me to a little holiday. These had been wedding gifts, and she always managed to buy them back, for they sit on my dining room table today.

With the third course of roast chicken, following a plate of ravioli, I am telling Tamar about significant moments in my parents' lives at Luchow's or Harry Bleak's, further uptown. How, one time, they encountered the publisher Horace Liveright just after Dreiser had thrown a cup of hot coffee on him. That happened at the Brevort. Or it might have been the Lafayette. Tamar does not demand accuracy, nor even the account itself. Something in her face tells me she is listening to an inner narrative of her own, a firsthand memoir and much more authentic. Before the meal, she had called the hospital in Ohio. The pneumonia seems to have been checked, but there are signs of liver failure. Tamar picks up part of her chicken and solemnly tears into the crisp thigh with her pearly teeth.

Several nights later, we walk around the Village, and I try to find Romany Marie's, but we end up in a chop suey joint a block from Louis's. After the fortune cookies, with what seem to be fatuously modest forecasts, we get over to Louis's, and Tamar heads for the telephone just as Zack walks in.

Zack graduated the year I entered the university and is a bit older than I and well on his way to becoming a successful hack. In fact, he is about to transfer his patronage from Louis's to the White Horse, and the rest, to use one of his phrases, is history. But at the moment, he is working for a skin magazine cutting out pictures of pin-up models, separating the breasts and buttocks and then pasting them up in various provocative layouts to illustrate the magazine's articles. I am happy to see Zack because he has spent some time in Cuba and supposedly had even got drunk with Hemingway a couple of times, though this turns out to be one of his better fictions.

"You look terrible," he says first off as he sits down. "What's the matter—have you been sick?"

"Not getting much sleep," I say. "You know, hitting the books." Then I tell him, all at once, about Tamar and about going to Cuba. "We made the reservations today," I tell him. And this is true. I phoned the airline from one booth in Grand Central Station while Tamar called the hospital in Ohio from another.

"For Cuba?" Zack asks.

"Yeah. Pan American. To Havana." I can't help myself and start to giggle.

Zack has nodded approval of the chosen airline, but he's not too familiar with the Isle of Pines. "Not as many pine trees as you might think," he does say.

"And they've discovered oil on the place."

"I have heard that is true," he says and sips his beer. "And this woman owns something there, you say?"

His interest pleases me. Usually, my role in this acquaintanceship is that of a loyal audience for the presentations of his success, of his chummy times with noted authors—what, for example, Norman Mailer had said to him only last week. So, I'm flattered by the attention he has been giving my theory about the workplace—how one's work is surely enriched by the long view. How the perception of one's culture can be sharpened, if not deepened, by living in another society. His eyes attend me closely as I speculate on the effect that living on a tropical island might have on metaphor.

Zack has been sipping his beer as he reviews my different theories and then he says, "A dream empowered can be a dangerous thing." He takes another sip and ruminates this wisdom. I am wondering if he's read it somewhere, say chiseled on the façade of a bank. But then he says, "Look at Hitler," and he leans back in his chair and hugs himself. "Not to mention the German people."

Then Tamar is back and sits down in the chair between us. She looks down shyly as I make the introductions, but she is obviously aware of Zack's intense study. Her ears and the edges of her nostrils have become rabbit pink, and there is a tremulous quiver along the line of her narrow lips. Maybe her husband has died, I think. We're off to Cuba tomorrow if that's the case. She has been on the phone longer than usual, perhaps making arrangements for the disposal of the body. I'll have to get my shirts out of the Chinese laundry on Amsterdam Avenue. I am busting to find out but can say nothing in front of Zack.

Someone has punched Clooney's numbers again and the familiar ditty rattles through the place. Tamar jumps up and leaves us as suddenly as she has arrived, like a bird lighting and then taking off again. She moves in her peculiar ritual before the altar of the jukebox, barefoot again. The new sandals are primly lined up on the floor beneath the table.

"That's the one?" Zack asks, his eyes level with mine.

"Yeah," I reply, enjoying his look. He shifts around to regard Tamar. She is slowly twisting in place, arms over her head and self-absorbed. Zack has verified everything. "By the way," I say, "do you know where Romany Marie's is? You know your way around the Village. Do you know what street it's on?"

Zack turns back. "It's around here somewhere. That's one of those old-time places nobody goes to anymore. That's one of those places you talk about like you were part of those old days. Like you have a history around here. You know, you are kind of ridiculous, trying to impress people with these names you are always introducing into conversations. You don't know anything about the Village or what's going on."

He gets up and moves to the bar and instantly goes head to head with another guy and the two of them are like secret agents or long-lost brothers. I have always envied this easy camaraderie Zack enjoys with others, for his being recognized already as "an old hand," but tonight I am filled with a pity for him that I do not quite understand. I do understand the accompanying exultation I feel.

My mother is now ninety-four years of age and lives in a nursing home several hours' drive from Pittsburgh. From my doorway here on Monterey Street, I take an easterly route to Altoona, where I turn almost due north to the town of Bellefonte. Talleyrand, my mother says, named the town during some tour of the new United States, perhaps when he was selling the Louisiana Territory to Tom Jefferson.

The territory beyond Altoona is very beautiful, a landscape that rises in undulant levels into the Nittany range of the Allegheny Mountains, and these long drives have become like retreats for me, isolated though movable studies where I peruse my memory's archives. Mile after mile, I come upon unexpected views, a turn of perspective, as the scenery changes.

Memory is a room always hitched to our travels, and, as we get older, its dimensions grow smaller so that certain artifacts are tossed out. We dispose of those items that no longer suitably furnish the image of a past we wish to keep; and if any clocks are kept, they are not kept going. Sometimes, this economy, this autumn cleaning if you will, makes room for totally new fittings, fanciful stuffs to refurbish a dark corner or redo an unsightly composition.

My mother is enjoying this kind of redecoration lately, which often puts her childhood days on the Panama on the same level with events she reads about in the daily newspaper. The journalist Vincent Sheehan, her university classmate of seventy-five years ago, is a contemporary of the late Senator John Heinz. She describes with great detail the memorial plinths being raised to both men; Sheehan's sarcophagus will be placed atop his column. Also, when she has moved things around in her memory, making certain substitutions, she finds the results often settle debts for services rendered her, as well as slights, and that these rearrangements in her memory often make it unnecessary to acknowledge a debt or even to express gratitude. *Please* has always been difficult for her to say and *thank you* nearly impossible.

Last week, she sits in her wheelchair and stares out through an immense wall of glass at the wintered plainness of the garden outside. We are on the ground floor of the nursing room, a large multipurpose room with a small library in one corner, television in another, and, near us, a large plastic Christmas tree. Tiny lights blink on and off. The ornaments are similar to those children might make and hang. Across the way, white-suited attendants are enjoying their lunch break, eating sandwiches while following a soap opera on the television.

My mother seems mesmerized by the barren prospect, her own being suspended in a kind of wonder at the still life outside the window. She resembles a Celtic crone, still not believing the spell that has changed her from the young colleen she really is inside, that has just changed her from the boisterous, fun-loving woman I can remember, busting into our house in Kansas City to tell about the sprees she and my father had supposedly been having in New York. The women across the way have not moved, caught up in their TV melodrama.

We have gone through the topics of our usual discourse: the poor quality of the food served here, the insensitive handling by some of the attendants, the condition of her bowels. From A to Z, so to speak. Sometimes I will throw a line into the subsequent silence to pull out a familiar story, practiced so many times that the parts of it slip into narrative with a worn carelessness. I feel as if I am attending one of those ingenious robots Casanova described that amazed eighteenth-century Venetians with their chess play until it was disclosed that within each was a clever midget.

Just to try something different last week, I ask, "Where was Romany Marie's?"

She blinks. The trance has been broken. Her large eyes turn upon me as her withered lip taste the air. "Why on Washington Square, of course. Washington Square South."

"No, it moved from there."

"It did? When did it move?"

"A long time back. A Gypsy place, wasn't it?"

"Yes, Italian Gypsy," she says and leans toward me. "When your father and I went there, it was still Prohibition. Marie made her own wine and would serve it to us in coffee cups, with saucers, so the police wouldn't find out." Her laughter is old and soundless but a youthful gleam has shot through her eyes, a triumphant glee.

"But you don't remember where the restaurant moved?"

"No. Why do you want to know?" Her mouth chews on the question.

I have no answer; in fact, I am trying to find that answer as I write right now. So, I toss another line into her memory. "What about Hitler?"

Her eyes become even younger, luminous. "Well, she and her mother couldn't get out of France because—you know. The Germans were going to put them in one of those camps. I knew if I could just distract the man they called Hitler, then they could sneak by." She leans forward and puts one arm behind herself, motions with her hand.

"So, you went up to Hitler and distracted him?"

"What?"

"You distracted him."

"I placed my little soft child's fingers on his hands and went like this with my finger tips. His hands were dry and papery to the feel. And she and her mother were able to walk behind me, past his police. While I did this with my fingers, I took this paper out of his pocket. When we got down to the shore, none of the boat captains would take us across the lake. But I showed one man the paper; he read it and then he said, 'All right. Bring your people on board.' And we got across the lake. On the other side was America."

"And you got them out."

"Yes, I got them out." The claim is modestly made. "But you mustn't let on that you know about this," she says and looks sharply at me. "It would embarrass her."

The mother and daughter in this adventure are a couple she has met in recent years who have extended many kindnesses to her. Even to this day, the daughter, a grown woman with children of her own now, cheerfully runs errands for my mother to the library or store and has been a regular and lively visitor at the nursing home. It is true that they fled the Nazis in France, for it is true that they are Jewish, and it is because they are Jewish that my mother cannot simply express her gratitude but must create this elaborate favor she did them, under the eyes of the ss Guard, and which they are only paying back with their different courtesies. Probably they will never be able to pay it all back because, after all, she had saved their lives.

My mother's job at the Bentley School started just as Hitler attacked Poland, and when she returned to Kansas City, her visits were full of endless accounts about her duties, the assignments she made. As I said, my parents had separated by now, so these academic reports substituted for the restaurant reviews we used to get. Moreover, these new stories were really for my grandfather's benefit. She rarely said anything to my grandmother and me if we were alone with her, but would idle in an impatient silence. She wanted to show my grandfather that someone was actually paying her money—a thousand dollars a year—for her intelligence, her education, and her ability. There, she could say; she was a success. But she would never be able to prove it.

As the war in Europe went on, her classes at the Bentley School began to fill with the children of refugees from Belgium and the Netherlands who had fled the Nazi blitzkrieg. They were well spoken, she said, fluent in English and several other languages—and they were Jewish.

"Diamonds and emeralds as big as your thumb sewn into their clothes," she said. "Oh they know how to take care of themselves."

Moreover, and to impress her father even more with the tests she faced every day, she could tell—just certain things, you know—that alliances were being made between these new people and some of the other faculty. Miss Bentley, the school's founder and president, was a sweet woman, but it was easy to see that she was being outmaneuvered. The atmosphere had changed.

Sometimes, after she returned to New York, I would lie awake in my room and imagine how it would feel to wear clothes sewn with precious jewels. Like chain mail maybe. And would they clink as you walked past customs, giving everything away? Such clothes would be uncomfortable, but her other remarks actually did make me uncomfortable for a reason I could not put my finger on—for the time being. I ascribed it to a kind of class consciousness, one student's resentment upon hearing a teacher speak harshly of other students. That my mother was the teacher made it all the more confusing.

Her efforts to prove herself to her father, then to her husband—which these suspicions of collusion only made more valiant—raised an enclosure around her sensibilities that was to keep everyone at a distance—even me. Even her grandchildren. She sits in her wheelchair, isolated by much more than her great age—an aged Penelope, redoing memory to set things right and even the score. Justice will be hers if not freedom.

"So, you got them out," I say.

"Yes." She laughs, again, at how clever she was. "I got them out."

The women locked up in the prison on Sixth Avenue generally provide a last diversion for people leaving the bars after closing time in 1951. Mostly prostitutes, they have been rounded up for the diversions they have already provided on the streets and in the doorways of lower Manhattan, and they trade insults nightly with revelers standing on the street below, shouting obscenities and other pleasantries through their barred windows. The exchange is almost a nightly ritual, but I attempt to walk Tamar past the crowd on the street, mostly men, and to the Anglia parked near Tenth Street. We had gone to Julius's earlier to hear some jazz.

But she pulls on my hand, and we stop. Some of the women shout down angry, vivid evaluations of the world in general and men in particular. Others get off funny observations that are cheered by the crowd. Some of the men shout up questions or add refinements to the curses raining down on them from the cell windows. One of the prisoners begins to sing and is joined, after a bit, by another from two windows over, and this sisterly duet momentarily quells the rumpus. "Blue Moon."

Tamar's face is suffused with a kind of wry perplexity, the kind of look Siennese painters put on the face of the Virgin during the Annunciation. Her blonde-lashed eyes are half closed as if she's looking up into a flare.

On the walk over from Louis's, she's been very quiet, inward looking, so I haven't disturbed her, haven't asked her about her husband. Perhaps I don't want to know? But when we go on to the car and get into it, she tells me without my asking.

"His condition has stabilized," she says. "There might be some kidney failure."

"Should we change the reservations? Put them off a little?"

"No," she answers after a moment. I have headed the Anglia down Greenwich Avenue, going west. "Let's keep our date." She leans toward me and places her mouth over my right ear. "Once," she starts another story, and her wet tongue stuffs each detail into my hearing.

Even with a couple of years in the navy and some time on a Washington newspaper, my sexual experience is mostly academic; that is, I have read more than I have done. But in the few days and nights I have spent with Tamar, my knowledge is becoming encyclopedic as one lesson groggily follows another. More than once, just when it seemed a syllabus had been fulfilled, she would whisper in my ear, "Sometimes," or "Once,"—in a sultry hour before dawn—and a whole new course would be introduced that unaccountably would renew my scholarship. Dimly, it has sometimes occurred to me that I am in the company of a peculiar Scheherazade whose endless narratives are not so much saving her life as draining off mine.

In fact, Tamar has so distracted me that I have shot straight across Seventh Avenue and now must continue all the way to Eighth Avenue. I tell her to sit up and watch the scenery. Certain of her husband's specialties, like his desire to rip up new clothes, I cannot afford, while others just don't appeal. I cannot bring myself to bite her pretty breasts as she has asked me to do a couple of times. But we have reenacted almost everything else the two of them had done in Ohio, which apparently is a much more worldly place than I have imagined.

When I make the turn at Eighth Avenue, Tamar has slumped down in her seat and seems to nap. Further up, we will pass a bookstore on the west side of the avenue, just below Madison Square Garden, where most of my recent sexual research has been done. The window of this store is crammed with sun-faded manuals on carpentry and back issues of *Popular Mechanics*, but inside, manuals of a different sort can be found: editions of classic erotica but all of them heavily censored within the proper limits of the 1950s. So, Aretino's *Life of Whores* is reduced to a flowery trivia; Nanna's advice to Pippa becomes nonsensical directions on pear cultivation—though an occasional metaphor slipped the censor's literal scrutiny. That gentlemen sometimes prefer "the back of the book" is an index that Tamar has already opened to me.

In this store, one could browse between the missing lines of *Lady Chatterley's Lover*, Frank Harris's memoirs and *Fanny Hill*, and other similar editions, forced to fill in the missing scenes with one's imagination, or, to give that imagination a rest, leaf through art books that contained pictures of Hindu temple façades, archival photographs of Greek amphora, or the naughty bookplates of Aubrey Beardsley. Lots of hair and pinched faces.

A hardcover series called *American Aphrodite*, whose editor was to go to jail for public obscenity, offered reprints of the *Kama Sutra*, the tales of Boccaccio and Balzac, and other curiosa that was in the public domain. The works of master engravers and artists accompanied these condensations. A timid selection of Giulio Romano's *Posizioni* fleshed out Aretino's poems, Rowlandson did *Fanny Hill*, and the austere prints of Fuseli popped up in a wide range of narratives. The prolific Perino del Vaga enjoyed a portfolio all by himself. Most of the Italian artists seemed more interested in the folds of drapery rather than the flesh within, and their lovers were heavy haunched and often caught in a maneuver similar to a pair of draft horses making a turn at the narrow end of the field. In fact, as we cross Forty-second Street, a few blocks from the store, Tamar has uncovered my caduceus, an exposure denied Mercurio because of all the bed sheets del Vaga wrapped around Glauros.

"I've got a test tomorrow," I tell her.

"In what?" she says after a little.

"Well, there's some disagreement as to when the *s*-plural came into Middle English. From the French, of course, but when? King Ethelred—known as 'The Unready'—married a Norman woman in 1002, sixty years before the Norman Conquest."

"A Norman woman," Tamar says reflectively.

". . . And that suggests French might have been spoken in the Saxon court before the Normans and Hastings. That she introduced the plural *s* ending."

"That's the test?"

"It's an essay test," I answer. We have just passed the darkened bookstore. On the curb before Madison Square Garden, what looks to be maintenance and cleaning workers are waiting for a bus or a taxi. The marquee is dark. Joey Maxim and Bob Murphy have fought it out but are still on the marquee, and the cleanup crew has finished sweeping up the aisles and washing down the toilets and is going home. The Nedick's stand at the entrance looks even more disreputable in the gloom; how can anyone drink that stuff?

The most contemporary illustrations the bookstore offers are small glossy black-and-white photographs of a model named Betty Page. These photos come in packets of a half-dozen poses, neatly wrapped in cellophane, with a different picture of the series on top, so that the economically minded browser can make a casual review of the whole set; perhaps on the way out of the store, after not locating the exact issue of *Mechanix Illustrated* he had come in for.

The photos show this raven-haired, sultry looking woman in a variety of uncomfortable positions. She is sparsely, yet completely, clothed in black underclothing with a black garter belt holding up black stockings. Her skin appears very white. She is sustained, if not suspended, in these complicated *posizioni* by turns of small rope that wind around her ankles, her arms, and wrists to terminate in knots of a simple excellence only to be found in a Boy Scout manual.

Moreover, the model wears glistening black pumps with heels of such a height that it is clear to anyone that if she had been able to break her bonds, she would not be able to run very fast. However, the expression on Miss Page's face suggests she has no desire to flee; in fact, she looks pretty indifferent to the whole business and, in most of the poses, looks out at the camera with a bored insouciance, like someone waiting in line at the unemployment office. In a couple of shots she exhibits a startled moue of the mouth as if during some of the more strenuous arrangements, on a chair or over a table, she has let go with a little gas. In several others she looks down with a post-Annunciation tranquility, a passive acceptance of her complicated and highly stylized fate.

But we have pulled up across from my apartment building. Tamar is ready to complete the maneuver that del Vaga had drawn a bed sheet across. "Let's get a little sleep," I say.

"This exam means a lot to you." She dips her head a couple of times to agree with her own observation. The truth of it is new to her. And to me. Her near-albino stare looks puzzled in the streetlights, a kind of bland appraisal. No disappointment, just the recognition of a fact. For the first time, she is really looking at me and she finds something amiss. Perhaps she sees her predicament for the first time.

I cram for my test as Tamar takes a long shower in the bathroom I share with several other roomers. She is a long time about it, for at this early hour of the morning there is plenty of hot water, and so I have fallen asleep when she comes back to the room. I am half roused by the delicious aroma from her delicate limbs, like new-mown grass, and her fragrant skin is pink and ivory. I fall asleep with images of her guiding her sheep into mountain pastures. I can almost hear the innocent, atonal clang of roughcast bells.

She sleeps through the alarm, and I observe her as I dress—one last possession. Her slenderness lies fully exposed in the morning light, the colors of her palette going from creams to rose save for her feet, where the callused flesh has become an ugly orange. I tell her I will be back with lunch and then lean down and kiss the blonde shadow of her triangle, a prospect, it seems to me, beyond any artist's rendering. She chuckles in her sleep, a knowing throatiness.

She is gone when I return. Today, the deli has given me lox as well as cream cheese, but she is gone. The new shoes have been neatly placed on the floor beneath the sink, and she has made up the bed. Pan American tells me the reservations have been canceled, but I could make others if I wished. They refuse to tell me if she has made another reservation in her name.

I have just remembered the title of that Chekhov story: "Dreams." Dreams realized can mock the dreamer, Zack had said the other night at Louis's. They can, to further employ his language, emerge from the dungeons of despair to create an unexpected tyranny. Look at Hitler, he had said. I am in Pittsburgh looking at myself going to Cuba in 1951, as I looked for a shortcut to being a writer.

Tamar had understood that I was not the Friday for her island, my footprints were to track on different sand. The cell of my room on 104th Street has become enormously empty and vast. I am pretty sure she has gone back to Ohio, back to her own imprisonment, leaving me to the dreadful freedom of the afternoon.

Chimera

A poet friend has sent me a collection of lines that were either cut from his poems in composition or that never made it into a finished stanza. He has assembled these lines on a page—all gleaned from different mornings' work and stirred by separate impulses—into a common cluster. Curiously, their meld makes a kind of sense, and their abandoned images sensibly come to life and find new homes in meaning. He calls the result "Out Takes."

Beside my desk is a large wire basket where I keep journals —some go back over two decades—in which I have recorded notes on my travels, reflections and observations, an odd recipe or two, ideas for a novel or an essay, the sounding of a joy or despair—odd threads to be woven into the seam of a larger work but which never found a place. My friend's salvage operation tempts me to do something similar, and I pull out a notebook from this pile beside me. The notebook's cover is worn and scribbled over (several anonymous phone numbers—who would answer in that past if I dialed them now?) and hangs loose from the wire spiral of its spine. I flip through its pages to come across this entry.

He had never been sure of her—never certain that she was telling the truth and that her lateness—her breathless tardiness was due to her lingering a little too long, he could not say lovingly, over some lummox in a motel.

Flushed from these recent exertions rather than from anticipating his company, her eyes still illuminated from recent frictions—he found himself accepting her on whatever terms she seemed to be offering.

Why? It was something unexpected, he reasoned, something rather ordinary that had become compelling. Say, the slight curve of her neck in the lamplight, as she read beside him, so touching, graceful and vulnerable; like the woman in Conrad's Victory.

Where did this come from? Is this fiction or the residue of an actual betrayal suspended in its own acrid gem of memory? I can't remember what was happening in my life then, who the woman may have been, and the pages around this entry are no help; they are mostly concerned with some of Ronald Reagan's cock-eyed economic policies. Maybe it is fiction. It's in third person and could be the fragment of a story never written that now lies nakedly, without context, on this notebook page. It doesn't read like a diary note, but is the objective voice only a mask put on to disguise my own feelings from myself? Who could this woman be, breathless and compelling? Have I made her up?

And lummox! Who uses words like that? The word only appears in the supplement of my Oxford dictionary, and it is cited as an American dialectical variation of the verb *lummock*, "to move heavily or clumsily." So, this melancholy voice envisions his rival as heavy and clumsy—read muscular and inexperienced—and the dismissive tone may be a defensive flick of the finger at a younger contender. The woman has lingered *over* the other guy—that's the adverb of choice—because the lummox is too heavy and clumsy to assume an active role. She's doing all the moving!

So what is the nature of this relationship that has been so betrayed? Reading side by side suggests a domesticity, a homey and comfortable place to which she arrives late and out of breath. Maybe not all that exciting, for reading is seldom put to the service of foreplay, but turn out the light and settle under the covers, she with a contented sigh and he shifting into acceptance. He wants her beside him no matter what the terms.

Are they married? Those breathless, tardy arrivals can also suggest she is joining him someplace public, probably for dinner, and these moments might be worn facsimiles of their earlier rendezvous, which were wild and slightly dangerous. Sharing a meal is a convenient device for a scene in fiction, and I'll say he's just about to finish the one martini he allows himself before dinner when she rushes in, her eyes brilliant with a light that eradicates the shadows that have begun to creep into him. Her quickness and bustle suggest youth; so I'll make her younger, which explains his patience and acceptance of whatever she gives him. It's part of the bargain he's made with time. But what does he offer her, what does she get out of this arrangement? Certainly a reading list, all those books she reads beside him. What about forgiveness for her missteps? That might draw her closer to him. Then there's wisdom, knowledge—aren't they supposed to accompany age? Lately, he's been steering her away from California chardonnays to introduce her to a St. Veran or the velvety rightness of a Sancerre. At dinner she digs into her food, chewing and talking cheerfully. She also likes to eat and has worked up an appetite. Several pages later in the journal, clearly long after dessert, and most of the page a crudely drawn map to someplace, I come across this item.

When they got inside the car, he held her close for some little time—enough to make her uncomfortable, he could tell. Not that she resisted his embrace or even objected, but its prolongation made her uneasy. She was used to these moments progressing, to move on to another, but he was apparently satisfied to stay on one plateau and without moving on.

So, on the way to his place—to break out the books—she is impetuous and eager to gain new experience and he wants to hold on to what he has. I am guessing that he is not so much satisfied with this "plateau," this new turn in their history that he may have just become aware of in the parked car, as he is more fearful of risking a new location—one completely empty of her.

"You're not going to tell me you've never done this before."
"I guess not."

I wrote down these lines in another journal, apparently while I was having diner in a small country hotel in the Meuse Valley. They are the same voices and several years apart, but I recognize them. I had put down my fork and took up my pen. But what's happening? She has sensed his anxiety and, good-hearted as she is, manages a palliative in the close confines of that car's front seat. After all, their dinner was sumptuous and the figs poached in red wine and topped with crème fraîche were out of sight. I know because that's what I had for dessert—it says so right on the page.

But done *what* before? The unattended pronoun teases the imagination. Her reply is whimsical, a kind of rhetorical shrug that matches that pell-mell entrance in the earlier note. The scant three words of her reply—"I guess not"—suggest a perfunctory pause in the proceedings, and the rest is silence. But later, toward the final pages of this same notebook, this musing is scribbled.

32

How sweet he found her deceptions, her superb technique with false-hood taught her by the many who abused her, that had left her wounded by the side of their brutish passage through her life.

Lurid prose and righteous anger, and all encased in a Proustian sensibility—read *The Sweet Cheat Gone*—but in all probability, whoever is talking may not be all that sorry about her "superb technique," and maybe she has not regretted the various abuses either. To credit him, he recognizes that he may be no different from all the others who have treated her so badly and that he shares the same bed, so to speak, with that lummox in the motel of the first journal. So, maybe this voice has some conscience, some awareness of what has been happening to them in the different pages. The insight may be more than he can take for he disappears from this particular notebook, and I must look for him through half a dozen others before I come across him again.

Like most men, he's separated women into different parts in order to understand the enigma only to find the puzzle even more unsolv-able.

Well, throw up the hands in Cartesian wonder—he's tried his best, tried his judicial best to understand this young woman, tried to put some clothes on the naked truth of this affair and finally understands it cannot be explained reasonably. If it cannot be justified, it's not his fault either. But on a page of directions through some villages in Languedoc, I discover the couple has reached some sort of accommodation to the fate my idle sketching has given them.

"Can you see Madame Bovary taking out the trash?"

"You mean packing up the garbage and tying a little ribbon around it?"

"Yes, something like that." Her voice had fallen. She had lost interest in the idea just now.

The light through the windows fell across the back of the chair as the light had graced her arms this morning as she raised her hands to adjust the coil of her hair.

Well, how did they meet? It takes me a long search through a pile of chronicles in the wire basket before I come across this clue in a kind of stenographic notebook. The rest of the pages are taken by notes for a novel never written.

The several references had been pushed to one side of his desk. He would get to them tomorrow. But he had been saying that for a month. He worried, a little bit, that the filing date on one had already passed. A student might fail to get an appointment, and would think her own inadequacies were to blame.

Oh, dear, this is beginning to sound like one more familiar account of an affair between a teacher and student, the stuff of academic imagination and a weary vita. Do we need another indictment of such foolish fondling? I used the plot myself in my second novel, An American Marriage, and I wrote that book years before I had even made up my first syllabus! Moreover, is it even the same young woman feeling inadequate? The same young woman who raised her arms in that other notebook to pose as a portrait by Vermeer in the morning light? That morning light indicates he feels somewhat responsible for her future, or is he just one more canny shark lollygagging in the shallows and ready to feast on uncertain minnows. Those earlier entries suggest him to be a man enmeshed and powerless in his own net, but sitting at his office desk, references pushed to one side, he is in control. He has become a power to be petitioned. At this point in most romances, a phone usually rings, but it doesn't ring until another notebook and on a page that also records a day's skiing in Colorado.

The French have all these idioms that you could never guess their real meaning—for example, "avoir du cul" is an expression meaning to be lucky. But its literal translation is—to have some ass.

Come to think of it that isn't too far off, he said to himself as he reached for the phone. It rang before he picked it up.

And it is she! I'm saying it is. She's calling to make an appointment. She knows he's very busy with all of his important projects—his monograph on *Madame Bovary* is still talked about in certain circles—but if he could just find time to write a couple of recommendations for her. So, she enters his office—his life—bearing forms for a Fulbright or some graduate program. She finds him, desk cleared; wise, patient, and randy.

The beads came from a bazaar in Tangiers, but she found them too heavy to wear comfortably. She worried his feelings would be hurt.

The first gift is rather ordinary and it shows up as a scrap on a completely empty page. Something he picked up at a tourist stall between panels at some conference. It is an ordinary gift from an exotic place, and that combination interests but does not alarm her. But it's too heavy for her neck; too heavy for a trinket and probably too garish to wear. She wants to be discrete—another reason not to wear it—but she's also worried about his feelings. The net is closing around them. Meanwhile, the recommendations have been written and sent on their way and the relationship has moved out of his office. They go on a picnic—at least somebody does.

It was cool here under the black pines, and the ground had the resilient feel of a mattress—not an especially good mattress but one that would do. She had already lowered the picnic basket to the ground and looked at him happily.

Something about her happiness in setting down the picnic basket makes me think this excursion was her idea. Privacy and distance from worldly bothers; she wants to play Eve restoring the Garden. What's in the basket? She's brought food she's learned he likes. A hard cheese of some kind, maybe an Italian pastore sini—that's popular here in Pittsburgh, too—crusty bread, a piece of cold chicken, fruit. Yes, and a bottle of wine, a red she could afford and not too grapey, she hopes. But she's forgotten a corkscrew—but of course, she knows he has his Swiss Army knife. They have become that intimate. Food seems to feed this romance; I find them on many pages chowing down. Here's a supper in a Chinese restaurant.

"Are you a dragon or a rabbit?" She had picked up one of the paper place mats with the Chinese zodiac printed around its edges.
  "Is this one of your sly ways of trying to figure my age?"
  "Come to think of it, you must be a boar."
  "How do you spell that?"

Yes, bore, indeed. Anxiety and moo goo guy pan don't make for an appetizing dish. But why does he worry about their ages?

Maybe he's begun to think this fling is becoming something more permanent, but if he keeps talking about it, she might start adding up their years and subtracting herself from the sum. She finds his worry boring and tries to make fun of him, but these cracks in his confidence bother her a little.

His whole family had been like that. Servants with a sense that they might have been really important but for a cruel toss of the dice. This attitude upset her.

He wasn't supposed to have doubts about himself—that was her department. His authority had drawn her to him, the heat of his assurance, but these peevish misgivings startled her.

Sometimes, he felt like old Monet with his long brushes dipping into the lily pond. It he could just tell the story straight out and without having to back off to bring it into perspective.

What story does he want to tell, and is this the voice of a writer, a different guy entirely? Also I'm startled to hear him whine in this different journal. Imagine how she must feel.

All along he had played by the rules, done his turn at the pump and held wire on the fence up for another to crawl through, but here he was on the wrong side of the fence and no one to help him.
Well, so what?

Yes, so what indeed, she might stamp impatiently. More sour apples. He's becoming tiresome, and these petty differences are accumulating in this pile of old notebooks. A line here, a scrap of dialog there, and nothing very critical by themselves, but when assembled they amass evidence of discord. Something has happened to those giddy arrivals, those innocent appetites in the woods. They have begun to have arguments.

"You will never understand me." She canted her head to fix an earring.
Was there something to understand?

Then, in another notebook, her voice pierces through some observations I was making on memory and Montaigne.

"You mustn't try to insult me—you don't have the wit for it."
"That sounds like Oscar Wilde."
"Maybe."

These two fragments, inscribed in journals that were kept years apart, create an unhappy scene when put together. She's fixing an earring in one ear, a final attention to her appearance after lovemaking, and they have begun to bicker. She's getting tired of him playing old Monet by the lily pond. Note the earring. Something tasteful in gold, maybe a loop, and far different from that tourist gimcrack he gave her before. So they have progressed from those early awkward exchanges to this serious entanglement. She's become elegant and confident and strong enough to stick him with the cool insouciance of an Oscar Wilde. He's taught her that, recommended the books anyway, and it doesn't matter whether it's a direct quote or a clever simulation. I want to think she's made it up. She's come into her own.

And who has this voice become? No longer the uncertain student, the beguiling lover. Who is this woman? *C'est moi, c'est moi.* I've read *Bovary* too.

I see more of that spirit, more of her independence standing up to him, in a passage in a shabby notebook held together by duct tape. He apparently has come to her apartment.

"I've had a rough day."
 "How about a drink. George Dickel, isn't it?"
 "How do you know about George Dickel?"
 "That's your drink, isn't it? I'm supposed to know these things."
 "Don't tell me—you have a lot of brands in that cupboard."
 "I don't do inventory until spring. If you're still around in spring, you can check the store."

This is my favorite excerpt. She's using that snappy, tough good-girl sound of a young Lauren Bacall. She's noted his brand of bourbon and that suggests her interest in him, and she returns his nasty remark with a warning shot that he better behave if he wants to know her better. The exchange suggests an intimacy, an affectionate familiarity, but when does it take place? She's living in her own place, and that means she hasn't moved in with him as the previous outtakes indicate. On the other hand, maybe she's kept her apartment, a wary gesture, as a place of refuge, and he sometimes comes there for a visit and they replay some of the old thrill of their early lawlessness.

But just a minute, what if I had picked this particular notebook out of the pile first? Encountering this little scene first—before that fateful afternoon in his office—would affect their relationship and require a whole new chronology. Every history is shaped by the order of its telling. Even in memory we make selections that configure the past, so the narratives of a single life can be contradictory and truthful all at once, reshuffled like cards and picked up and played out as different hands.

One thing is certain—this couple is not always together, and in several pages he shows up at night alone. Her absence is un-explained. No quarrels are evident, and he looks into the dark silence around him.

The city continues to grow up around him, so at certain hours before daybreak, lying sleepless in bed and the windows open to suck in the early hour chill, he was sure he heard the sound of its growth, reaching like a strange algae up the outside walls of his building.

He's having a panic attack, a figment of a horror film; he's alone and hears his own mortality creeping up to smother him. Apparently no air-conditioning either. If she were in the picture, lying beside him—reading of course—she would wool him about it, tease him and make him laugh at these shadows on the wall. And sometimes he does tell her about his dreams.

One morning he could swear he could smell his mother's apple pies baking in the apartment building. In some unit, his mother was pulling three or four pies out of someone's oven. She had got into the apartment somehow—the occupants were at work—and she had made these pies. Now they were done, and she would tidy up and leave. But here's the joke. She had thought she was in his apartment, and she had made these pies just for him—she had come back just to bake these pies as a surprise for him when he returned from work and found them. He would know that she had been there, that she had come back. But she had gone into the wrong apartment and—just to continue the nightmare—he would go from door to door, floor to floor, trying to find the right apartment, The one with the pies.

Misplaced affection. She knows all about that; after all, it might have been one of the reasons she had sought him out in addition to those letters of recommendation. This kinship they share moves her, moves them beyond the mere semblance of a semester's romance, and she wants to hear more of his dreams. His attempt to heal the wound in a dream, however ironic, appeals to her. He becomes the storyteller and she likes to hear about his life—how he was before they met. It's more interesting than any of those books he's been recommending. And he's right here next to her.

As a boy he enjoyed swimming long distances in a good-sized lake where his uncle ran a bait and tackle shop. Round and around, he made the circle, imagining he was Johnny Weissmuller with every stroke of his arms raising cleanly from the clinging water and then slicing through its surface with little disturbance.

This image of him swimming appears in a small notebook; almost vest-pocket size and some of its pages torn out. (What story has been destroyed there?) The episode strikes her with the clarity of that pervasive light that sometimes falls upon her neck. She can see his arm raise "cleanly"—surely a Hemingway adverb—then "slicing" back into the water to imply the neatness of a superior swimmer. The language excites her also—he's introduced her to this arousal—as does the picture of him as a boy practicing the same qualities that have attracted her to him as a man. Effort and strength combined with grace warm her, and now she has seen them in an earlier version of him, and this perception somehow grants them a curious longevity. A history before it unfolds. She keeps this insight to herself, stores up its knowledge in the same place she keeps his preference in bourbon.

But who's kidding whom? Her observations about his swimming as a boy could just as easily be reflections that he wants to think she experiences—he's put them into her head. Or someone has.

Silences will always fall between them. Here's one in a last journal, a final turn of page.

Again it was as if he had come to the banks of a great river, like the Mississippi, and though there might be a bridge, even ferry boats toiling back and forth, his crossing would still be an event, an act that would leave certain familiar faces behind on one bank and encounter strangers on the opposite shore.

"Penny for your thoughts," she murmured.

"They'll cost you more than that."

She pulled herself up and kissed him on the mouth. "There. Paid in full."

"I was thinking there's a piece of pie left and how good it would taste with a scoop of vanilla ice cream."

Food again. They read and they eat, and he has moody thoughts. They reside in the wire basket beside my desk, caught on pages between segments of my idle perceptions or maps and directions that no longer lead anywhere. I'll leave them alone to sort out their own narrative, to tell it from any direction. Or not at all.

In My Orchard

My orchard here in Pittsburgh consists of two apple trees, a pear, and a peach. These are small trees, developed in a nursery as dwarfs of the species, that I espaliered against the brick wall of my neighbor's house, since to allow them to grow to their natural shape would make an impenetrable jungle.

The technique of this two-dimensional horticulture was practiced by the medieval gardener when the security of the walled manor came first and the cultivation of fresh fruit was secondary. The supple shoots and limbs of a young tree were trained to follow a trellis fixed against a surface so they grew flatly, and the different designs of these arrangements were as various as the imaginations of the growers.

For the peach trees—and I had two at the start—I chose a pattern much like the arms of a menorah, rigging the design with stout nylon cords threaded through eyebolts screwed into the brick wall. Year after year, I carefully led the pliable limbs of the trees along these lines, tying them off at certain points and gently bending them to the left or to the right into the ninety-degree turns that put them on a perpendicular course. For the apple and the pear trees I chose a pattern called *vertical cordon* and its name gives its description.

The trees dutifully followed directions and grew wonderfully, and within a few years we enjoyed fresh peaches picked within feet of Mimosa Lane where the city's garbage trucks were known to rumble. The apple and pear trees seemed hesitant to bear fruit, but as I went about this modest, first harvest it amused me to think that I had reproduced a moment in this city backyard that had been shared by a medieval family hundreds of years before, who in turn had regenerated this scrumptious import from the fabled orchards of Araby. One delicious bite of a peach connected me with that history, and surely the trip was similar to the effect of that nibble of a cookie in a certain fin de siècle Paris drawing room.

So vanity as well as fruit had been cultivated, as within a family when all seems going to plan and where offspring follow a determined course, making all the right turns. The child's fruitful performance ennobles the progenitor—his wisdom and character are embellished as his agronomy is verified. I gave no credit to the peach for its deliciousness nor did I recognize its efforts growing through the mannered course I had laid out for my own gratification.

But something went wrong. One peach tree began to falter, losing leaves at the bottom of its trunk while the crop at the top became minimal. It resembled an injured athlete, determined to complete the race and hobbling toward the finish on the strength of instinct alone. The leaves became mottled by ugly growths that no nurseryman could identify or at least recommend a remedy. Then the leaves fell, the limbs atrophied, and the tree died.

Nor did the apple trees bear fruit, though their blossoms were many and their leaves glossy and healthy looking. But the pear tree did produce fruit—one. This single pear hung in the center of the tree, and the heavy foliage of the apple trees on either side made a bower for its stunning appearance. I watched it take shape and color over a season as its first pip gradually swelled into the feminine form of its maturity. The cool greenness of its youth softened into a lemon yellow that deepened as the fruit grew larger. I feared a bird might peck at it or a prankish squirrel knock it from its limb, but the pear continued to grow untouched and hung like a small lantern in the depths of its greenery. One day, as I lightly measured its sensuous curve, it fell into my hand.

The purity of its shape, the unblemished texture of its golden skin declared its perfection—it was genius and invention all in one. Too good to be eaten it reminded me of a rare vintage wine that should only be laid down and never opened, growing more valuable with each passing year. But there was no way I could stay the inevitable rot that had already begun its course at its core. I showed it to my wife and neighbors. I wanted somehow to send it to friends or even fly them in from different parts of the country to see this ultimate pear, and if any made fun of its singleness, I would suggest that one perfect pear might be sufficient. The tree had bent all its efforts to produce this single flawless specimen, and what more could be asked of it? What a cruel destiny (as well as a handy metaphor) for excellence to be achieved only to be consumed in a moment's hunger. The fruit was sublime, sweet and juicy, and the tree has borne no more.

But on further reflection, the yen to seek metaphor put aside, it became clear why this single tree produced only this slight harvest, for pear trees require cross-pollination, and in my ignorance I had planted only one of them. From where had the pollen come to instigate this particular germination? None of my neighbors in the central-north side have pear trees, and we are many miles from suburban yards, too far for an errant bee to navigate. Something carried on the wind, perhaps—an immigrant gamete that landed by chance on my pear tree and flourished. That random coupling was the remarkable event.

Meanwhile, the stricken peach tree had succumbed, and as I dug up its dead root one spring morning, the branches of the other four trees leaned forward as if bent in grief. But of course it was the sun that drew them from their wall moorings; the power of its attraction had even pulled some of the eyebolts from the masonry. Simultaneously that morning sunlight also illuminated my folly, my ignorance and impatience with proper method, for, without thinking, I had planted these trees against a wall with northern exposure. The sun only attended them fully in the late afternoon. Opposite, on the line I shared with my other neighbor, the sunlight was continuous from morning to night, but only a chain-link fence marked this boundary. I could have erected wooden trellises there to support the trees but my imagination had been limited by the images of medieval walls and the romantic allusion of growing goodness within a sanctuary. I had ignored the sun's compass, and it was a wonder that any fruit had appeared on these branches at all. The prodigious effort that had produced that single pear became even more remarkable, even heartbreaking.

Now, the remaining peach tree has been stricken with the same disease that took its companion, but the top branches— those most available to sunlight, my dumbness has finally perceived—blossomed to produce a couple dozen extraordinary fruit. This top-heavy bounty was meant to teach me a lesson, I think; a super-arboreal demonstration of what could have been done if I had only been sensitive to the tree's needs. If I had not denied it sunlight.

Thus, my stewardship has been put in a bad light also. Within the urban confines of my backyard, only my witless conceit has flourished. We know that out of mean environments, phenomenal progeny can occur, but how that happens begets its own thicket of theories. Years ago and in another life, I planted fifteen thousand conifers on a hillside in upstate New York. They were tiny fledglings of red and white pine and larch procured from the state conservation service, and it was very hot work. One daughter brought me glasses of water during the days of my labor and the other child helped me place the seedlings in the slits my spade made in the earth. I saw myself as Dr. Astrov in Chekhov's "Uncle Vanya," creating and bequeathing this forest to future generations, and if I were to be known at all it would be for this wood in Columbia County—that would be enough. How noble!

The summer heat made me dizzy—though it could have been the vapors given off by my sweaty ego—but the trees took root and thrived. They grew to impressive size as the children also grew and went their different ways, as I also grew apart from that hillside. Later a blight struck the red pines and they withered, turned brown, and today reportedly stand like dry sticks. The forest I had planned to leave for others has become a field of tinder.

My friend Jeffrey Schwartz, an anthropologist, has posited that we descended from the tree-living orangutan, and this ancestry may explain the special affinity we have for trees. It is an attraction not without some apprehension—a walk in the woods can refurbish the soul as well as threaten the body. The wilderness is important in our history and literature, as singular as a clump of cottonwoods rising above a lone prairie farmhouse. To be under a tree and feel its rough bark against our backs is to center ourselves in the universe. We build tree houses and ravage forests, and some of us attempt to make orchards in our city backyards.

This spring one of the apple trees is bearing fruit. Its limbs are loaded with small green apples, and their jolly shapes, their daily increase in weight, bring the tree's limbs lower and lower, reaching out for more light. This pose of supplication may also pardon my careless husbandry.

Making It Up

My copy of *Robinson Crusoe* is an edition published in 1887 by Estes and Lauriat of Boston, and it was given to me by a man named George Iles on August 28, 1935. Mr. Iles lived a couple of floors above my father's rooms at the Hotel Chelsea, and he had befriended me as I rode up and down the hotel's rickety elevator—one of my pastimes on those summers when I traveled from Kansas City to New York; when the season seemed to turn my father, mother, and me into a traditional family unit.

> Hilary Masters from George Iles
> with every confidence in his success
> New York, August 28, 1935.

Mr. Iles's celluloid collars were of such rigid construction around his thin neck that I often expected his spectacled head to pop off like a cork from a bottle, but his formal attire in the elevator was a disguise for the bibliographic chaos of his rooms. Books. And then more books. He was a collector of books, and their jumble went from wall to wall and, to my seven-year-old wonder, all the way to the high ceilings. Laid up like bricks, the musty volumes formed a maze in which I could get lost as I inhaled the toxic fumes of their ancient bindery, became mesmerized by the embossed calligraphies along their spines. I walked through aisles of literature, and to this day my mind automatically puns his memory when I encounter the word. What I'm saying is that Mr. Iles provided me a stunning sensual experience, and though the transfer of knowledge upon innocence can become a scarifying episode (sometimes with profitable consequences later as a dreary memoir), this Edwardian gentleman's seduction left me only eager for more ravishment; a normal life forsaken. Mr. Iles's gift of *Robinson Crusoe* made me a writer.

Back at my grandparents' house in Kansas City at summer's end, I came down with whatever infection was making the rounds of the second grade at Scarritt School. Let's say chicken pox. Quarantined to my bed and strengthened by my grandmother's ox-tail soup and egg custards, my incurable boredom turned me to the brownish volume only just unpacked from my suitcase. "With twenty illustrations by Kaufman," the title page fraudulently claims, because there are no pictures and no evidence that any had ever been bound into the pagination, but my initial disappointment was quickly overwhelmed by the first sentence.

> I was born in the year 1632, in the city of York, of a good family, though not of that country, my father being a foreigner, of Bremen, who settled first at Hull: he got a good estate by merchandise, and leaving off his trade, he lived afterwards at York, from where he married my mother, whose relations were named Robinson, a very good family in that country, and from whom I was called Robinson Kreutnaer; but, by the usual corruption of words in England, we are now called—nay, we call ourselves, and write our name, Crusoe; and so my companions always called me.

Whew! Talk about convoluted prose and cluttered punctuation! But the coils of language, the lassos of references held me face to face with several intriguing likenesses. *Though not of that country*: what country could I claim? Kansas City? New York? *My father being a foreigner*: my father was a strange figure to me, a mysterious man of puzzling importance whom I only saw in summer. And to change one's family name called up a recurrent fantasy that I was an orphan and had been adopted by this kindly old couple who kept and fed me nine months of the year. The status of illegitimacy was not within my seven-year old ken, but the sense of the condition was.

Moreover, the confident, first-person voice that speaks so casually and candidly from the page beguiled me. Trust and belief are immediately secured. I could hear that voice, carried it in my mind; a plain sound but sometimes with an offhand guile that tickled me with its timbre, a note later to be identified with irony. I was hooked and flipping through the early pages; their headings only drove the fluke deeper: "Misfortunes at Sea," "Captured by Pirates," "Escapes from Slavery." The man had a natural tabloid talent for grabbing a browser's interest. And these incidents some thirty pages before the famous shipwreck on the deserted island off the coast of South America were where my ultimate corruption, procured by George Iles, would commence.

But, in the meantime, Defoe's own story strikes out on its interesting course. Perhaps, an excusable divergence here. It should be comforting to all of us who dare to write to know that this progenitor of the modern novel was something of a hack. He was born around 1660 (different biographies give or take a year), but almost thirty years after his fictional creation. He also changed his name of Foe to Defoe, thinking the Frenchified version had a little more class. Good for business. His father was a butcher who urged him toward the pulpit, along with the fairly good education that went with the calling, but young Daniel wasn't called, preferring to set himself up in the hosiery business. In the seventeenth century, it's to be remembered, probably more men wore stockings than women, and the incipient author did well for awhile, trading in Spain and Portugal, traveling through France, making it in London. Then his business failed and he declared bankruptcy, but his political interests had been sharpening his quill in the meantime, eventually to change his course again as it was to affect our literary forms.

Born the year after the Restoration (Milton was still alive, blind and fuming), the ex-hosiery salesman pulled on a variety of opinions as a pamphleteer. He was enormously prolific—some count over three hundred tracts, pamphlets, and essays published under his name, not to mention the scads of journals he wrote for anonymously or edited. He somehow escaped punishment for his participation in the Monmouth Rebellion, but he did serve time twice and was even pilloried for his published opinions on religious freedom. He was convicted of libel once. His tracts ranged widely, advocating changes in highway construction, prison conditions, bankruptcy laws, and even recommending higher education for women. His ideas were usually far in advance of the period and often got him into trouble.

A satire called *Memoirs of Sundry Transactions from the World in the Moon* is said to have given Swift the idea for *Gulliver's Travels*, while *A History of the Plague* amply proves Defoe to have been a first-class journalist. He had an eye for detail, he was a man on whom nothing was lost as Henry James might have said, but more times than not, his eye was on the mark because he wrote for money, for advancement, and would take on any point of view that paid for it.

A satiric ode defending the Dutch king William against the xenophobic whine of the Jacobites attracted the attention of the royal court, and Defoe was appointed the royal mouthpiece. While in this cushy post, he also wrote anonymous anti-royalty pieces for the Jacobite journal *Mist*, but recent scholarship suggests he was serving as a double agent in much the same way the CIA infiltrated the left-leaning editorial policies of *Encounter* magazine in the 1950s. Nor did he neglect his domestic rituals, laying down his pen now and then to father seven children. He became very prosperous, with a fine town house and a country estate, but was to die under mysterious circumstances in 1731, having spent the previous year in hiding for reasons still unknown. However, a dozen years before, in 1719, lightning struck him at the age of fifty-eight.

Or at least a meeting struck him. It was with one Alexander Selkirk, a sailor who had actually been marooned on a deserted island and who apparently handed over his journals of that experience to Defoe. No surprise that this classic of fiction is based on an actual event—hasn't that always been the case? Of course, lately, the written life comes to us unadorned by invention, plainly out of the fire, uncooked if not unleavened, and hastily served to appetites that prefer the dish not so much deconstructed as unconstructed. We seem to have lost the taste for reality put together piece by piece; perhaps a final counterrevolution against modernism's piecing, but that's another digression for another time.

So concludes this brief synopsis of Defoe's extraordinary life, some of which was to be found in the introduction of my Estes and Lauriat edition, but prickly with chicken pox, I have no mind for it as I suffer confinement on Roberts Street. Especially because I have by now reached page 31, "The Ship Strikes upon the Sand." Here the magic commences, as does my apprenticeship.

The morning after the storm that has wrecked the ship and drowned his companions, Crusoe wakes on shore with only a pocketknife, a pipe, and a tin of tobacco. He swims out to the hulk, pulls himself aboard, and starts to put together the reality of his next twenty-eight years, two months, and nineteen days.

He begins to make new entities, fabricate items from a salvaged past. First, a raft made of broken spars and planks to transport the usable stores he can find aboard the derelict. Corn grain intended for the chickens that had perished. Muskets, powder, and shot. Some tools, clothing, rum, and cordials—these last from the captain's cabin—this is all he was able to bring ashore that first day. In an irony for which we must credit Defoe, the ship had been on a slaving venture, so that its small cargo was composed of trinkets intended to trade with "Negroes" for other human beings—mirrors and strands of beads and such—all useless for a man trying to survive on an island. Except for the crates of hatchets, that handy item of hardware for which many a tribe bartered away its land and existence. Crusoe brings off dozens of these.

The issues of slavery and colonialism hinted at in these early pages and to be amplified in the person of Friday later, can only be briefly mentioned here to avoid a digression from the headway I'm trying to make. Because, in the meantime, Crusoe has made several trips out to the wreck, bringing back canvas sails, lengths of chain and rope, pens and ink, Bibles of both persuasions (but never to crack one of them), shovels, needles, thread—even the ship's dog swims ashore with him on the second trip as the crew's two cats gingerly cling to the bobbing raft. Bit by bit, he has assembled the materials to put his life together, piled them up around himself on this uncharted shore, all the ingredients for survival—to make a good story. He even creates more company for himself, in addition to the dog and cats, by training a local parrot to talk to him, teaching it to say, "Poor Robin Crusoe. Where are you? Where have you been? How came you here?" thereby lending the bird a droll insight into the human dilemma it might not have come upon if left to itself, eating nuts and berries.

Downstairs, my grandfather Tom Coyne rattles the glass panels of the bookcase and takes out a volume of the *Encyclopedia Bri-*

tannica—let's say volume 7, "Damasci to Edu." But he's looking up "Diesel," not "Defoe," or maybe he's turning to "Dredging" or "Docks." This self-educated immigrant is obsessed by such research, and he glories in human invention, not the least his own. He had studied civil engineering by army correspondence school while riding herd on the Sioux, and he had put this minimal book-learning to practical use building railroads in Mexico, Central America, and Peru. To read about the mechanics of human ingenuity and effort somehow reflected the picture of himself that he so vainly tried to hang in the American gallery.

For it was with such pieced-together knowledge and hard work that my grandfather confronted the hazards of this wilderness on whose shores he found himself at the age of fourteen, cut off from his family and his native Ireland. With no identity. Isolated. To say he coped would be an understatement though the word's primal meaning describes his constant struggle, a continuous setting up of defenses against the unknown and the unseen—even within his marriage and paternity. The continual preparation and repair of defenses is the life's work of the immigrant; it is a castaway's regimen even though an enemy may never show up. The labor of putting up walls, of making the fortress sound, becomes more important than the fortification—even its purpose is lost. Moreover, to erect a fortress around a property—if only a picket fence—is to define the property and make it more valuable, which in turn reflects upon the value of the work involved. Indeed, if no enemy threatens, the worth of the defense has been proved and the work of it justified as well as its cost. Working hard is the success story of the alien—no other reward is really necessary and, in any event, is rarely handed out.

The stakes and pales that the industrious Crusoe hews and pounds into the ground around his domain make such a fence, never to be attacked, though he fears the natives who occasionally barbe-cue their captives on one of his beaches. The first of these picnics is the occasion when he rescues Friday, but it is Crusoe who at-tacks the natives—a peremptory strike we might call it—slaugh-tering them with the instruments of his imported technology: the flintlock musket and pistol. But he is never satisfied with his security and constantly builds more fences, each new stockade enlarging his holdings, as if he doesn't have the whole island in the first place. It does not occur to me, at age seven, that the subtext of *Robinson Crusoe* is work, nor that this castaway shares the fear of being unrelated to his surroundings that all outsiders fear—like Tom Coyne downstairs reading the encyclopedia. The construction an exile puts upon his reality not only is meant to defend the particular plot he has staked out, but acts as a sort of tether that keeps him from floating away from it.

But I do remember wondering why the man never took up fishing, a much easier source of food than the hard-scrabble farm-ing he threw himself into. A never-ending supply of food swam just off shore, but of course that would have been too easy. He planted and harvested corn, barley, and rice, learning how to con-serve seed and manage his crops. He gathered and dried grapes to make raisins for winter meals. The wild goats that fortunately inhabited the place were domesticated for meat and milk. He even taught himself how to make butter.

Obviously these are slim pickings, not the usual tropical island fantasy or the la-la land Odysseus sometimes washed up upon, but the isolated province of a philosophy which preached that acceptance by a community, not to mention the Almighty, only came through hard work. Defoe surely carried the rigors of his Cromwellian youth, but the lesson was lost on me, my imagina-tion awash in Defoe's quick-paced narrative.

The twenty-eight years plus pass in a couple of winks—one

event comes fast upon the other. The guy could tell a good story, and he keeps the action moving continuously. No modernist he, and the reader is given little opportunity to reflect or look around the narrative and wonder about time and space. Also, sensual details are totally absent, for Crusoe seems to have lost his appreciation for beauty along with his identity papers. He may look at the ocean, but it is to study its currents and tides, not to glory in its metaphysical splendor, and there isn't a single description of a sunrise or a sunset, and they must have been humdingers.

But that doesn't matter. I am caught up with the details of him putting his life together, as the story is put together, and my grandmother worries that I am straining my eyes. She's heard that certain childhood diseases can affect the eyesight, and in a way, she is right, for I will never look at the world the same way again. By now, the shipwreck has planted a large square post on which he notches the elapsed time of his abandonment. He invents a method that keeps track of weeks and months as well as days. His habitat consists of a reinforced cave and a second home for the dry season—a country estate if you will—made of the ship's sails. He's discovered how to fire the island's soft clay into pottery for storing grain and boiling goat stew. He's built boats and takes up tailoring, using the dressed skins of animals. He's rather proud of the jaunty cap he's designed and sewn together—just a little vanity left over from pre-Cromwellian times—so he's not a complete drab. He bakes his own bread, making up a way to grind the corn and sift its meal, and then he puts together an oven from fired clay bowls heaped over with hot coals. He must do without yeast, but then he's not making Wonder Bread—the process itself is a wonder.

Once Friday runs pell-mell into his life, escaping consumption to become a factor of consumption, bells begin to ring in my fevered head. I had just read *Huckleberry Finn*, and that young exile's journey down the Mississippi, and with his own Friday, seemed very similar to the one I am reading, written two hundred years before. The raft that Jim and Huck shared was a sort of island set adrift, and they were left to their own resources to make do. To make up their identities. Surely, there must be a ton of theses somewhere on this likeness. But there is a difference. Twain backs away from the conclusion toward which his feelings are steering him, for his courage or his venality got him no further than the stunning metaphor for our national predicament, and maybe that's enough. But Defoe finished his novel with Crusoe continuing as the wandering loner, especially after Friday's death, to head out for the territories of China and Siberia, to return to England at age seventy to prepare for his "final journey," emphasis on *prepare*.

But another lesson has been teaching my imagination. I had already pictured myself as an orphan, set adrift nine months of the year from my parents; perhaps a prince forced into mufti. Kansas City was not quite a desert island, but something told me it wasn't where I should be. And here, in *Robinson Crusoe*, I came upon the plans and the methods to reconstruct my reality, to overcome my sense of isolation. Defoe was loaning me some of Crusoe's tools to create my own shelter and circumstance. The shipwrecked sailor showed me how to bring together scraps of happenstance—how the debris of the past and the present can be salvaged to make up a different identity, a new worth in the work of its own making.

In Rooms
of Memory

Recently, I picked up this old book from a stall outside a used bookstore in Pittsburgh's Squirrel Hill, and as I held it, a certain remembrance slipped from its pages though I had never read the novel: *The Walls of Jericho* by Paul I. Wellman. The book has no jacket and its boards are of a maroon color. A striking illustration, perhaps in a pen-and-ink wash, decorates the end papers. The picture leads the eye along the perspective of a half-harvested wheat field and into a small town in the distance. The standing water tank and an assembly of grain elevators—a windmill on the outskirts—identify the place as a prairie community. I know this place; that is, I remember passing through something like it on childhood journeys to visit cousins in Topeka, Kansas, my grandfather at the wheel of the Buick. It is always a hot and dusty excursion from Kansas City, and my grandmother sits in the passenger seat, fanning herself with a program from last night's Democratic Party meeting, where she had been one of the principal speakers. Yes, I remember all that, and I remember the moment as if it were yesterday, as the saying goes.

But how much of that memory is imagined? Thomas Hobbes argued that imagination and memory were one and distinguishable only by the names given them. But was he suggesting that the one makes the other—that all memory is composed of fancies that have slyly taken root around the recollection of a moment like the chickweed that appears around the trunk of the lilac in my garden? Lately we have become obsessed by the loss of these images as if the weight of them has become more than ageing sinews can bear, while the energy to create new simulacra wears out. Perhaps we are born with these images already seeded within us and, one by one, they mature and wither.

Also in the book's illustration, the horrifying tentacle of a tornado has just touched down in the outskirts of the village, and the density of the black cloud from which it descends suggests power enough to take the whole town to Oz and back—water tank, grain silos, the one church steeple and all. These prairie tornadoes have Old Testament awe about them, as terrifying as they are spectacular. They resemble the furious return to the Earth family of some member who has been banished. I remember them, too.

But I do not remember this old novel, so why do I hear my mother's voice say, "Yes, *The Walls of Jericho*. It's worth reading. About Kansas." Because of her endorsement made on the street before the bookstore, I buy the novel, and the guy seems happy to take my dollar.

But when did my mother make this recommendation? When do I remember her saying it? Was it during one of her own returns to my grandparents' house in Kansas City, where I grew up—an impassioned return, if not furious, and bringing us tidbits of culture from New York City? These items were shared with us, accompanied by the cracking of chewing gum or the emphatic crunch of raw vegetables between her canines. The sound of that savage consumption snaps in my mind even as I write these words.

This novel now on my desk was published by J. B. Lippincott Company of Philadelphia and New York in 1947, which would be five years after that living room on Roberts Street—where I thought I first heard her praise this novel—had ceased to exist. By 1947 I had been taken east for the rest of my life, had finished high school, begun college, and seen service in the navy, so if she did make this recommendation, it wasn't made in Kansas City. I have imagined the place incorrectly.

Wellman knew the place he imagined as Jericho, though he made the town up. The writer was born in the Oklahoma panhandle and finished college in Wichita, Kansas, earning some of his way as a cowhand. He had also attended high school in Utah where he absorbed the history and culture of the Native American. He began his writing career as a journalist, first in Wichita and then in Kansas City as a reporter and editor on the *Kansas City Star* in the 1930s.

So, here's a connection between that living room on Roberts Street where I remember my mother holding sway and the author of this secondhand novel about ambition and love in a prairie community on the edge of the twentieth century. They were also the same age; Wellman a year older than my mother, and it would have been not improbable for them to have met. Often on her whirlwind returns, she wangled invitations to speak to some group endeavoring to foster culture in Kansas City, say, the local chapter of University Women. The subject of her address would be my father, perhaps a recent book of his, and I can remember her rehearsing one of his poems in the bedroom she used on these visits. She hammered the lines of a Homeric ode to Oliver Hazard Perry's defeat of the British on Lake Erie in 1813 into the oak moldings and thick plaster walls of my grandparents' house as if they were parts of its construction that had been omitted. Later the membership of the University Women would be similarly nailed to their seats by her stentorian timbre, and this moment is clearly imprinted on my mind for I am sitting in the back of the room, brought to the occasion—another trophy.

So, as I say, it was not improbable that the *Kansas City Star* would write up the occasion—Wife of Famed Poet Addresses University Women.

And one of its reporters, even its managing editor, might attend to check her out. At this point, let's say 1937, Wellman had been thinking of giving up journalism for full-time writing—fiction. After all, a writer named Hemingway had preceded him on the *Star*. Like most small-town wannabes of that era, he felt *Winesburg, Ohio* had been written just for him, and here, showing up, was the wife of the author of *Spoon River Anthology*, which had inspired Sherwood Anderson. He must have been curious to see what she was like.

What she was like was a black-haired, green-eyed Irish ex-flapper with a loud laugh on her and a fierce swipe at a world that shunted her aside because of her gender. A picture of Wellman used by the *New York Times* for his obituary in 1966 shows him to be of regular features, nothing remarkable but for a mystical gaze outside the photograph's margin, a kind of far-sighted humor in that expression that reminds me of my old friend, the poet Winfield Townley Scott. Wellman would die of lung cancer, so I suppose he may have been a heavy smoker.

Actually, in 1937 when he could have turned up at that afternoon gathering of culturally concerned women, Paul Wellman was already a published writer of some merit. The Macmillan Company had done two of his studies of the Old West, *Death on the Prairie* and *Death in the Desert: The Fifty Years War for the Southwest*, and just the year before, also his first novel, *Bronco Apache*. These books, the nonfiction still kept in print by the University of Nebraska Press, had been preceded by articles on personalities and events of the frontier era in scholarly journals like the *Kansas Historical Quarterly* and *Chronicles of Oklahoma*. Curiously he published some of these early efforts under the name I. Wellman, dropping his first name and substituting the initial of his second as if to separate this persona from the journalist at his daily grind at the newspaper. Or it may have been only a kind of bookkeeping to keep the different genres in separate files.

In these books, both the novel and the nonfiction and all that would follow, Wellman brought the materials and knowledge from his own youthful history wrangling herds on the near limitless plains of the early decades of the twentieth century. The hard toil and ever-present dangers of that work imbued his prose, whether academic or fiction, with an authenticity that would attract the interest of Hollywood, always looking for a scrap of the genuine to stitch into their patterns of make believe. In 1944 he gave up journalism and moved to California to become a screenwriter for Warner Brothers and Metro-Goldwyn-Mayer, contributing his store of firsthand knowledge to the making of numerous westerns. His production of books also continued at a prolific pace. By the time of his death, the Library of Congress Catalog lists forty-eight copyright entries under his name, fourteen of these novels, many of which were made into big-picture westerns only a year after publication. He also produced a biography of Senator Stuart Symington of Missouri in 1960, in all probability a work commissioned by that politician during his flirtation with the presidency.

"It's worth reading," my mother's voice tells me as I stand beside the bookstall on Murray Avenue, holding this old copy of *The Walls of Jericho*. But where did she make the recommendation? Not Kansas City—I've already discovered that. Place in either fiction or nonfiction is enriched, as Paul Wellman must have known, by observed details that stimulate the imagination. The squeak of a saddle being cinched, the changing color of a western desert—he drew components like these from his memory and put them into particular parts of his novels or his movies. But such details can be lifted from their original site and put down almost anywhere; they have no allegiance and are promiscuous. At the same time, memory itself is a place we move through as if through an immense storage bin where the miscellaneous pieces of our journey give dimension and character to the premises. They are available to dress a scene, validate a story, enforce a belief; their utility is unlimited.

So I'm saying my mother made this recommendation in 1947 when the novel appeared, and somehow, after her death and fifty-seven years later, the endorsement was repeated as I picked up the book in Pittsburgh. But where did she say it originally? In 1947 I was still in the navy and visiting my parents intermittently in their cramped apartment near the women's junior college outside of Philadelphia, where my mother taught literature and composition. The two rooms and hallway on the second floor of this old stone farmhouse were owned by the school and came with her job, and it was a surprisingly cozy and commodious lodge for my father in the last several years of his life. Add to their complement my grandmother, brought east from Kansas City and out of the desertion into which my grandfather had cast her on his way to the Valhalla of the Soldiers' Home in Washington DC. She slept on the sofa in one room that was also used for meals and for my parents' evening reading and for my mother's schoolwork. The hallway had become a sort of kitchen where my mother made meals on electric hot plates.

So that's the place, but it is rather bare, so I will haul out some particulars from my memory; say, put a jade Buddha on top of the bookcase, a spray of dried witch hazel in a copper vase, and then the rasp of the lawn chair when my father's weakened knees let his weight drop into its seat. The ordinary mortises of wooden chairs had been pulled loose. Those times I returned on leave, I would sleep on the sofa of a colleague's apartment on the third floor. I've set the scene.

I'll guess it was in one of those two rooms in 1947 where my mother would say, "*The Walls of Jericho*. Yes, it's worth reading." But what would have prompted the remark? Her reading list those days was composed of the literary classics she was introducing to her students at Ogontz Junior College: *My Ántonia, Pride and Prejudice, Bleak House*. Maybe she had read a review of the novel. The *New York Herald Tribune* Sunday book section said it "was difficult to put down." The *New York Times* credited Wellman with "painting a full bodied canvas," though the reviewer felt the climax was overly melodramatic. The *Saturday Review of Literature* also gave the book serious consideration.

I can imagine a Sunday afternoon in 1947, all of us in our different places in that small apartment, reading the Sunday papers. My mother would come across a review, say in the *Herald Tribune*, and she remembers Paul Wellman from ten years back in Kansas City when she gave that talk to the University Women. Hadn't he come to hear her, introduce himself, and do a quick interview—wife of the poet? It was a role she often played and in many places, so why not in my imagination?

She wouldn't know that *The Walls of Jericho* is Wellman's fifth novel, but I can hear her tell my father, "Yes, he worked on the *Star*." She adds, "It's about Kansas." My father always regretted he was born in Kansas, so he merely grunts in response.

Wherever this endorsement took place, it has hooked me, and I have begun to read the novel. Wellman begins the novel down at Jericho's train station where the protagonist and many of the town folk await the arrival of the evening train from the East. Dave Connors is there to greet an old friend, Tucker Wedge, who is returning from a newspaper convention in Illinois. He publishes the local *Clarion*, and he is returning with a wife.

The locomotive headlight hunted toward them in the dark. With hiss and clank and the splintering ding-dong of a brass bell, the train pulled into the platform.

The metaphoric verbal "hunted" quickly engages me in this scene, as both reader and writer, as the two friends meet and the newspaper editor introduces Algeria, his new wife. She is not especially pretty but has "an elusive charm" and wears her costume with an "elegant witchery," with eyes that "seemed almost to crackle with some hidden determination."

Look out, Jericho, here comes Algeria! She's the stranger, the odd element introduced into this small city in western Kansas that has been mostly concerned about the weather and the year's wheat crop, but this newcomer will change everything. So far so good; the narrative is started by the standard ignition common to all story telling, and I slip comfortably into its worn familiarity.

That "hidden determination" within Algeria's charm is quickly revealed in her ambition to gain her husband's nomination for Congress, which pits him against his friend Dave Connors, the county attorney, whose candidacy has been supported by local farmers and other folk. Algeria is not so much interested in political power as she is in getting away from the dull drawing rooms of Jericho and into the glittering salons of Washington society. So, Wellman adroitly plays the old theme of a woman's fascination with trivia affecting both a friendship and history.

The novel became a motion picture the year after its publication. It starred Cornel Wilde, Linda Darnell, Kirk Douglas, and Anne Baxter two years before she was to portray the cunning Eve in *All about Eve*. John Stahl directed the film, and he was also known for

Leave Her to Heaven and *Magnificent Obsession*. Film buffs credit him for originating what is known as "women's films."

The two friends become bitter adversaries, Jericho is torn apart, and into this division comes Julia Norman—the bright, fresh-faced, and lithe daughter of old Judge Norman, wise when sober. She has also become a lawyer since she left Jericho as a tomboy, and she and Dave Connors become lovers. His marriage has become stale and made even more unbearable by the presence of one of the all-time most hateful mother-in-laws in contemporary fiction. With gossip and scandal, violent deaths, political chicanery, and malicious journalism, Wellman seasons the stew to produce a satisfying, happy ending, melodramatic as the *Times* may have found it. But throughout the novel are passages of considerable power in their creation of place. Here is Julia viewing the landscape from a train window as she travels west.

The rich, tree-embossed earth of eastern Kansas was far behind. Moist plowland, and groves of elms and oaks, were back there somewhere along the endlessly parallel gleam of steel rails. Here, the train seemed to crawl across a featureless country, low hills in the distance, yellowish and apparently sterile, yet covered with summer-cured buffalo grass. The country seemed abandoned. Here and there a few cottonwoods struggle along the crooked water courses, emphasizing rather than diminishing the poverty of the soil. An occasional settler's cabin appeared remotely.

At long intervals they passed through little hamlets, desolate looking and afflicted with a dreadful sameness. Frame depots, water tanks, grain elevators, thriftless stores along deserted main streets. They were identical in almost everything, even to town loafers leaning in the shade, talking idly and spitting tobacco juice.

This moment and others just as compelling were drawn by Wellman from his memory and relocated in the novel's narrative—a train ride across an imagined prairie. He included the small detail of the settler's cabin to give dimension to the immense sweep of the panorama, but the image of that shack may have come from his own experience as a young man taking a train to Wichita and college. As a mature writer, his imagination called forth these details from his memory to invent a picture on the page that I looked at recently at the behest of a voice remembered from a room in my own past.

When we say a person's memory is failing, what we often are witnessing is a revision of history in progress that is often meant to redress a remembered wrong or fill a void not in memory so much as in that actual event—to make things come out right, appear sensible. In her last years, my mother would come upon a gloss of truth in the deepening loam of her dementia, mica of her own making, that illuminated or justified some past behavior or made a connection to link the different rooms of her life. Our imaginations endlessly tinker with the plot even though we can never change the ending.

My Father's
Image

This morning in Villefranche-sur-Mer, a low layer of nimbus covers the harbor, softly chased by a discrete sun. Beyond, Cap-Ferrat stretches out to enclose the rade like the arm of a sleeper, and just over its shoulder of pink-roofed villas clustered in pine woods lies the village of Beaulieu where Chekhov visited in 1897. A black schooner loafs on its mooring below. Today is my birthday.

I think I must be the same age, sixty-eight, as my father was in the picture that just arrived by fax from a publisher who asks my permission to use it in a school text. The electronic transmission has bleached out all the textual subtleties of the original photograph, so he is barely on the paper. Only the circles of his glasses distinguish the roundness of his head, and the ghost of his torso rises into the space of blank paper where the black trapezoid of a necktie floats unattached. My fading remembrance of him must fill in the slant of shoulders, the muscular arms, though perhaps my eyes have been fooled as memory is always shaded by nostalgia.

He is seated, a hand silhouetted against the book it holds, and I am standing beside him. I look to be about six or seven, though I am dressed much older—made up like a miniature adult and probably for this picture session. I also wear a necktie that has become, in this reproduction, a striped missile, and my left hand curls into a half-fist against the dark swatch of long pants—a nervous, uncertain gesture perhaps fetched by the unfamiliar scratch of material against my bare legs. Or maybe it was the formality of this moment of record that bunches my fingers; possibly being posed beside this man, my father, whom I rarely saw and hardly knew. He seems to be regarding something outside the picture.

Yet, the overexposed quality of this reproduction has left the remains of a smile on my child's face, though the dimples we both share have become invisible. My head is slightly turned down and toward him, a sketchy cant of affection, even a curious interest, emphasized by the shadows of my boyhood's long eyelashes. This morning on the Cote d'Azur, my eyes strain toward a second sight, no more to be trusted than any other, to fill in the blanks left by an indifferent electronic signal and generate the feeling in that room of the Hotel Chelsea that summer's day in, let's say, 1936.

Almost forty-nine years ago this man, so scantily arrayed in his chair, died, and even then his likeness was far from complete. Today if I attempt to call up a picture of him in my mind, he takes on the appearance of a character actor in an old movie, in black and white and before Technicolor—someone like Sidney Greenstreet or, more suitably, Charles Coburn who, in fact, had been a friend and bar chum at the Players Club and even helped produce one of my father's historically thickened plays.

I visualize this father character making entrances and exits in his rooms at the Chelsea, lighting and relighting his pipe, hunched over his desk covered with papers and manuscripts there or in a farmhouse rented for the summer. I would be brought east from Kansas City to perform in both these settings, almost like an extra for a scene, and later, when he became confined to a chair like Lionel Barrymore, it was I who appeared and disappeared during leaves from the navy or during university breaks.

So, our turns together on the same stage were brief, certainly improvised, and for reasons I've already tried to understand in a family biography.

The person who had dressed me so formally for this picture was undoubtedly my mother. The original photograph appeared in an article in a New York newspaper—a feature on the aging poet and his young family doing the city sights. Together. My mother's image does not appear in the piece, though the photographer must have wanted to take her picture as well. Raven haired and vibrant of expression, she was an extraordinarily good-looking woman, and at thirty-six, her beauty had reached its zenith. But she preferred to stay behind the scenes, as she often said, though she had usually stage-managed those scenes—these photo opportunities as we say nowadays—as if to prove to the world that we were a family. Her Irish pride would permit nothing less, but I've come to suspect her shyness was calculated to stimulate an attention she professed to abhor. After all, she had been of the theater.

But my inquiry this morning, this washed-out likeness of my father and me on the table beside my portable typewriter, has to do with that "search for the father" as Stanley Kunitz puts it: that ancient quest all poets seem to talk about from Homer on down. In my case, I have both much and little to go on. The facts of his life (not always accurate, but who am I to argue) are available in numerous reference tomes, in critical essays and monographs, and in a biography now being written. The poundage of his own written output bends several shelves in my library, and his diaries are packed in a safety deposit box. Letters and journals and unfinished manuscripts spill from two steamer trunks in storage, while a much more extensive collection can be accessed in the University of Texas Library. A lot of him is all down, on every page and in every footnote, but these documents that give scholars a familiar acquaintanceship are useless to me.

Nor can I piece out his person from those accounts recited by my mother over the years, because her narratives have been shaped and reshaped around a will to consecrate their union, to ascribe to it a nature it never possessed, while hiding—either out of loyalty or pride—her own wounds in the light of his genius. When young, my questioning of her was too timid, and now dementia has reduced her likeness of him even more than this fax before me. In fact, he has completely vanished from the screen of her memory.

So what I am left with is secondhand, abbreviated, and possibly just a paste-up at that, while what is missing is the sensual aura of the man: the smell and feel of him, the handling and warmth of him on a cold morning, the rub and texture of his ordinary stubble. All children, but especially boys, I think, need to come of age within the embrace of an adult male or else they might seek that domain in strangers later—or sometimes, turn that search into metaphor. The relationship of father and son has its own sensuality, its own special eroticism which requires satisfaction and which, happily in my case, was supplied by the hard immigrant's mentorship of my maternal grandfather, Tom Coyne, who raised me in Kansas City until I was fourteen. Yet, a scrap of that hunger has compelled me to attach myself to older role models, no doubt to their alarm; senior writers such as Kunitz whose poetry so movingly weighs this same loss. His father committed suicide before he was born.

So the pangs are reawakened from time to time, as this old photograph has done this morning. The date cannot be discounted. My birthday. As Montaigne has taught us, the only record we can truly verify is our own, so perhaps I carry within my personal album a picture of my father that is far more complete than what I have sought fruitlessly elsewhere. My children are now distant from me geographically, as they say I was to them even as I passed through the rooms of their childhood, and perhaps now they can only visualize a faint transparency of the solid figure I thought I was. They have the advantage of miles of home movies and family snapshots, but these are mostly of them and allow only a fleeting glimpse of this wily shadow, their father. After all, I was the photographer, so I'm absent from these pictures with a couple exceptions—striding down our driveway in Hyde Park, New York, or at the wheel of our little sloop off the coast of New England. Another bit of stage-managing like my mother's? The motivation may have been the same: to preserve a history of children and their mother, a midcentury middle-class American family going about its daily minutiae, but without the father. Even that John Wayne imitation strolling down the driveway was rigged—I had set the camera on a tripod and filmed myself automatically.

Surely they were as stung by my absence as my father's perplexed me. I excluded them from my attention and imagination in the same way my father kept me from his hotel suite, exiled me to Kansas City. It is Christmas Eve, and I am almost fifteen. My mother has sent me up to his rooms as she waits downstairs in the hotel lobby; they have been living apart for several years. I am on Christmas break from boarding school, and my mother has determined that this scene be played out, part of the tragedy she keeps running in her head. Something from Euripides perhaps. My father speaks to me through the partly opened door. His face is peculiarly sectioned. I cannot come in. I cannot stay with him, this night. He celebrates with others. So I return with my mother to her meager corner of an apartment shared behind a bookstore on East End Avenue, my chagrin hardening into a resolve never to make such a foolish errand for love again. Similarly, my children must have looked vainly for me as I peered at them through the viewfinder.

Where is Poppa, they must have asked each other, though I was in the room with them, sitting in the library of the old farmhouse we shared in Columbia County. My attention was elsewhere, just outside the picture. Why is Poppa mad? No doubt my anger was felt, spilling over to scald them or their mother with a look, a silence. Honesty about the past, to paraphrase St. Augustine, may be about all we can hope to achieve in the present; therefore, let me admit belatedly that this rage was against myself. I had only been looking for a clean, well-lighted place in which to work and had somehow walked into this bourgeois cell that seemed to stifle me.

The children of my father's first marriage must have felt a similar numbing chill that hissed from the weld he had attempted to make of his two selves. On one side, the successful lawyer who appeared briefly in their rooms to kiss them good-night, a respectable Chicago burgher who then sat down to dinner served by maid and butler. While behind that silent screen projection ran the wild unedited footage of a prairie wannabe. He saw himself as Apollo forced into a three-piece suit, and he knew that he had gone to the tailor on his own. Oh, I can savor the delicious depth of that self-pity and feel the scourge of it biting him!

One daughter would never forgive him this deception. Another would spend her life pursuing the same muse in the hope of encountering him someplace in that wood. His son, my half-brother, responded to the betrayal with ire made indelible, permanently souring him. Yet, his filial need was so strong, as if sickened on the very food it desired, that he could never blame his father but lay about with broad swipes, even to include my mother falsely for breaking up that genteel household. But I digress.

Those three children and I grew up strangers to one another, though bonded by the sightings we made of the same apparition. Later, my own children were to join this frightened circle. All of us can tell each other the same ghost stories, for the specter that haunts me, that vaguely manifests itself on this fax on my desk, is of the same species that walked away from them and down the driveway. Out of the picture. One abuser breeds the next—we know that now, whether it be individuals or peoples, and so it must be with fathers. The taste for a father denied makes for an appetite never fully satisfied in others, in work or ambition. No amount of picture making or posturing can assuage the sensual hunger.

My own hunger sometimes seeks its fill in dreams, not an uncommon phenomenon. Some years ago, the aroma of my father's pipe drew me half awake. The familiar smell of the Prince Albert tobacco he favored circled and hung in my semiconsciousness, and without opening my eyes, I knew he was standing at the foot of the bed, contentedly puffing and observing me sleep. I could visualize him, no need to open my eyes, though he had been gone from this world many years. He watched over me and seemed pleased by how I had turned out, and I snuggled down beneath this watchful love like a child, comforted by his sentry. The blessing I had sought from him in life, he gave me in a dream.

So, on this birthday, I make this wish: that I crawl back into my father's arms to feel his abrasive, unshaven cheek on mine, and then that I reach down and gather up my own children and hold their sibling sweetnesses tight, giggling and skewing on my lap. We will be like one of those antique monumentals of togetherness, generations scrambling over each other. Perhaps this old anchorage outside my window brings such antiquities to mind. The ancient Greeks dropped anchor here to trade and plant their olive trees while telling stories to each other of errant fathers.

In Montaigne's
Tower

For Wayne Dodd

It is, as he writes, exaactly sixteen "paces" across the thick pav-
ing stones of the circular floor. Two large windows are set into
the curve of the stone wall to look out on the garden below and
the landscape that falls away from this high butte on which the
chateau was built. Greek and Latin inscriptions use the ceiling
timbers of the room as a commonplace of collected wisdoms, but,
of course, the bookshelves that Montaigne had carpenters fit into
the stone radius of the outside wall are long gone and the beloved,
well-thumbed volumes they held put into national archives.

It is Wednesday, the first of May; a sunny, cool morning that
can almost be savored on the palate like the crisp, fruity Entre
Deux Mer from the vineyards nearby. The city of Bordeaux, of
which Montaigne was mayor in the 1580s, lies about fifty kilometers to the west. The chateau's caretaker is my casual guide, and he
has continued to describe Montaigne's regimen in a manner that
indulges my hobbled French. *Voici*—he walks to a far diameter
of the room—is *le trou sanitaire* that the Master had masons open
in the medieval floor—an innovative bit of sixteenth-century
plumbing so that the calls of nature would only briefly interrupt
the composition of an essay. On the opposite side of the chamber,

77

another vent connects this tower study via an airshaft to the family chapel three floors below. Montaigne could remain scribbling at his desk and still hear the daily masses celebrated there.

My guide's right arm sweeps up and around in a wide windmill motion as he delivers what seems to be an often-made but no less worn observation. His Gascogne expression is only slightly lifted. Yes, *je vois*, I nod; I get the idea: spiritual inspiration rises from below on one side to infuse the genius at his desk, and then the waste of this exchange is disposed through the opening opposite. He offers the procedure as a kind of basic model of creativity. *Aussi, c'est practique!*

This pilgrimage made to my master's snug retreat has also been a journey to satiate, once and for all, my appetite for France. Some of us may remember *les pommes frites* of the late 1940s. Plump slabs of potato sautéed in olive oil and shallots, sprinkled with parsley, that accompanied a *biftec* that was often *plus cheval que boeuf*. This cut of frites has all but disappeared, replaced by anonymously extruded perfections—deep fried and common to restaurants and road stands across the republic. But yesterday I stopped for lunch at a Rouliers on the outskirts of Nicole on NII3 to eat with truck drivers. Roast pork had been the *plat du jour*, and the tender slices of meat were accompanied by hand-cut chunks of potato sautéed crispy brown around the edges, redolent of garlic and sprinkled with chopped, fresh tarragon. Prefabricated spuds have yet to come to that part of the Lot-Garonne.

But I digress, for it is not only the food and wine that have mapped this ramble up from Provence and along the Garonne River. I have come to that time in my life when a return visit to a favorite place on earth will probably be my last view of it, my last taste of it. For instance, all the idling meanders I have made up and down the Meuse Valley, along the old battle lines of that horrible slaughter that shaped my century, have bred a melancholy passion for those fields of grain that indolently stretch out in the brilliant summer sun of Lorraine, beneath the dark-green shoulders of the Argonne. The awful carnage that occurred there, its horrors muted by time, season my understanding of human idealism gone astray, remind me of how greed and stupidity can pollute the best intentions of men and women.

And here's another idea, surely preposterous in its vanity, that in these places—this Dordogne Valley for instance, where at certain turns of the road I encounter an earlier self—I might leave something of myself behind. Maybe years from now in some of these villages the guise of my figure turning a corner will be confused by a resident with another. So, once again to digress, I seem to be talking now about memory, that two-way mirror we all carry of the past and before which we adjust our histories to fit the present. I don't recall that Montaigne ever specifically writes about memory, not even in any of his digressions, and this is curious for a man who so immersed himself in the bound volumes of antiquity. Perhaps his time was so consumed by the present, by its current events—the Reformation with all its attendant barbarisms to cite just one—that the sixteenth-century "now generation" found no space in its reflections for past events, for memory. Montaigne's father, Pierre, was born only a couple of years after Columbus had discovered the New World, and that astounding happening was still making front-page news in Montaigne's day, stimulating him to write one of his better-known essays, "Of Cannibals."

So it is these memories of France, this glut of its past, that have partly driven me here to give homage to Montaigne, while satisfying once and for all this craving that almost amounts to a strange jealousy. It is no wonder that Montaigne and his contemporaries, such as Shakespeare and Cervantes or Copernicus and Galileo in science, were so brilliantly glib—they had brand-new material to write about! To fly to the dead orb of the moon and return is an amazing feat, but only that. On the other hand, to return with stories of an alter world populated with people much like us, who are going about their odd religions, raising zinnias, and putting the Julian calendar into stone steps—now that's the stuff of supermarket tabloids! Some inspiration! It is like the past catching up with the present to make an entirely different here and now. These days it seems we mostly write of what might have been, and our significant characters are all has-beens.

"I am overwhelmed by the past," Wright Morris will say to me. I am now on another pilgrimage, this one to California, and he has just met me at the door of his apartment in a retirement facility. Yet, when I follow him into the room, I am thinking of Montaigne's tower. Wright's comic, complex intelligence that has so enriched our literature, and the understanding of our literature, through his essays, is losing sight of its own perimeter to become almost as seamless as the inner wanderings and wonderings of his characters in such novels as *Field of Vision*, *Ceremony at Lonetree*, *Works of Love*, or *Love Among the Cannibals*—to cite only some favorites from a huge bibliography. The astute focus on things, on moments that "tell all," effortlessly hones the conversation, but the *all* these things are supposed to tell has mysteriously eluded identification, fallen through the witty schema. A dry Nebraskan humor still edges the droll appraisal in the blue eyes; it is the look of a prairie-town barber who knows all about Pascal and Henry James but isn't so sure his customers should hear about them. Not just yet. "You see what is happening here," he will tell me with an uncanny objectivity. "This isn't what I expected."

It is as if time, which he had used so skillfully to arbiter his characters' inner lives, has lost the hands of its clock though the mechanism continues to function. Past and present are all one, real and unreal undivided. "I knew who you were, Hilary, when

I came to the door, but which Hilary you were out of the pasts we shared, I did not know."

Last night I stayed in a small family hotel in the village of Branne. Montaigne's tower is only open to the public for a few hours once a week on Wednesdays, and I have arrived on Tuesday, the last day of April. At the *hotel de ville* in Castillon-la-Bataille, I was given directions to St. Michele de Montaigne, the tiny feudal hamlet established to serve the needs and security of the manor family. My Michelin tells me that Castillon received its distinctive title from a battle fought here in 1453, in which the English lost control over this part of the Aquitaine, an early demonstration of the real being separated from the unreal, which the British are still having problems learning today. But I digress.

My hotel is situated on the banks of the Dordogne River and at one corner of the village's covered market. In fact, when I open the window shutters in my room, I look directly out on the river, which is fairly wide and fast flowing at this point. Here also, a modern steel-truss bridge spans the crossing, probably a replacement of a stone bridge destroyed during one of the century's battles over the ownership of this territory. Almost due north from my window, at a distance of about eight kilometers, are the heights of St. Emilion, and I promise myself something from that domain at dinner.

And it is a Chateau de l'Arrosse of the grand cru, rich in Merlot that Mme Proprietaire decants for me in the hotel's plain dining room. About ten tables are placed correctly upon a gleaming wood floor, each with a small vase of blossoms, a kind of petite lily, set precisely in the middle of the white paper table covers. Windows overlook the roof of an adjoining building and toward a slice of the river beyond. Two couples are already into their first courses as I taste the wine. They are of about the same advanced age, but one couple seems to be local citizens having a night out at the town's hotel. I had seen them earlier in the establishment's bar, having their *apertiv*, and they had been included in the family-like gossip—the give-and-take of the place. The second couple, seated near me and travelers like myself, speak a peculiar language that turns out to be Flemish.

"You speak French very well," the man says to me in heavy English. I had only ordered the eighty-franc menu from the timid young woman someone apparently has pushed out of the kitchen to take our orders, so this compliment on my language skills puts me on guard. Am I being conned? I lightly tap the shape of my billfold within my jacket's breast pocket, but then I put them together with the large Mercedes that is parked next to my little Peugeot in the market square. In addition, the authority of the man's polished baldness suggests respectability. They are, in fact, art dealers returning from a business trip in Spain to Belgium.

My duck is crisp and tasty and served with a pureed medallion of something that could be turnip, and its musty root flavor plays off well against the sweet pungency of the fowl. Mme Proprietaire has brought her young son, a boy of about three or four, into the dining room to greet the guests. The child, guided by his mother, makes a solemn tour of our three tables, offering his hand with a large-eyed frankness. I met his father in the lounge before dinner, just as the man returned from his daytime job. He had put his lunch pail down next to the bar sink, rolled up his sleeves, and took up the gossip and the servicing of the locals as his wife left to attend kitchen matters. The art dealers have been trying to engage me in conversation, mostly their complaints on the state of contemporary painting. They say that all worthwhile work has already been collected. My mind is elsewhere, and has no place for their dilemma.

Montaigne's tower was closed today, but I had been able to visit the ancient, small church of St. Michele in the writer's village. A local resident had shown me the crypt behind the altar where the writer's heart is buried. Whether at his behest or by his widow's sympathetic direction, I do not know, his heart was placed alongside the remains of his father in September of 1592. The rest of him was entombed in a cathedral in Bordeaux only to be moved about in the next several centuries in a ludicrous pawn game run by prefects, archbishops, and academicians. But his heart remains next to his father in his home village.

We know something about that relationship. A robust seigneur of the Renaissance, the elder Montaigne trained servants to wake his baby son to the strains of harp and flute. Moreover, all the help who served the young child spoke only Latin to him and he to them; he heard no French until his fifth or sixth year. Pierre Montaigne, something of an early environmentalist, introduced his son to animal husbandry and a respect for all animals, for the miracles of plant life and the cultivation of the vineyard and granary. The arts of war were not neglected, and his father showed him the handling of weapons and armor, for the young noble would need this expertise if he were to serve his king and protect his estate. In this last curriculum, horsemanship was the important course of instruction. Under his father's tutelage, the two of them often riding side by side into Bordeaux, Montaigne learned a lifelong appreciation for horses—a pleasure in the power and movement of a good horse under him even when enduring the awful agony of kidney stones that attacked him late in life. He writes that the inspiration for many of his essays came to him on the back of a horse, contrary to the theory suggested by my guide at the tower. "We can't afford to take the horse out of his essays," Emerson was to write centuries later.

I read of this companionship, so intimate and resolute even in death, with a mixture of wonder and envy. My own father, separated from me in life as well as death, lies in the small village of Petersburg in central Illinois—his "heart's home," he called it. No part of me will ever join him in that rural graveyard for our destinies have put us on divergent paths; yet, he did pass on to me some important lessons. Not in horsemanship, for sure. No Latin and less Greek, but an affection for the ideas and literature born in those languages. A love of music, though I have not his heavy taste for such composers as Brahms and Dvorak. My skepticism of certain human endeavors and pretenses—such as altruism—is a reflection of his thinking. But books, keeping a library—there's the connection.

To my wife's agitation, books are piled on our tables, spill in heaps from stuffed shelves, and lie about the floor and on chairs like spoiled pets. I have a miser's greed for books, and I pick them up at random to read a passage or follow an argument or inhabit a poem. I carry them from room to room, portable transitions of thought, of the past into the present, only to put them down in a maddening disorder. Guests sometimes ask, "Have you read all these books?" My answer must be no. But they are there for me to read, or reread someday. If I am to have wealth it is in my books, and when I regard their spines pressed together on the bookshelves, observe the casual sculptures they make on a table, my spirit becomes cozily furnished.

My father's love of books can be measured by the depth of his anguish caused by the loss of his library in the course of his first marriage's divorce. In all of our meetings, my visits to him in New York City, the loss of that library invariably entered his conversation. By then, of course, he had collected other volumes of Homer, Goethe, Keats, and company, but these were reproductions, so to speak, and did not carry the imprint of that first handling, the scent of that first enthusiasm. Over the years, he would write the son of that marriage pleading with him to find some way to return the books of his library to him, but the son always claimed vague difficulties; he could do nothing. After my father's death, the son revealed he had had the library all along, and, in fact, he donated the library to a collection and took it off his taxes.

So, in this modest dining room of this small hotel in Branne, I have been taking account of these quite different relationships between fathers and sons: one so ardently physical, using Aristotle's empirical methods to learn of the world, and the other distant, coolly intellectual and seeking worldliness in books. It must be evident that I have nearly consumed the St. Emilion, for, together with the silky surfeit of a crème brûlée, my senses have become transported, reality addled and sentimentality ascending. I yearn to fit myself beneath that bony cheek in Illinois.

"All the Rembrandts in the Hermitage are fake," the art dealer says. The Belgium couple finish their coffee and leave.

This morning their big gray Mercedes has gone when I throw my bag into the Peugeot and drive across the Dordogne to retrace the twenty kilometers east toward St. Michel de Montaigne. The tower and its companion at the opposite end of a stone rampart are all that is left of the chateau that Montaigne knew. The main building was destroyed by fire and rebuilt along the same lines in 1885. However, the portal is the same one Montaigne used, and the family chapel on the ground floor of the tower was unharmed. A mural on the wall behind the small altar shows St. Michel subduing a dragon within the lion paws of the family crest. A fresco trompe l'oeil around the walls attempts to suggest a larger diameter for this cell.

The second floor contains a bedroom where Montaigne often spent the night, too weary from creating this new form of literature to cross the courtyard to the family chambers. Even the name of this genre was his invention from the French verb *es-*

sayer—to try, to test. Then, the top floor, this large circular garret with a much smaller alcove sporting a fireplace. Winter quarters for the essayist. On one wall of this room, he had painted the declaration of his retirement on his thirty-eighth birthday: "long weary of the servitude of the court and public employments, while still entire . . . to the bosom of the learned Virgins." That is, the Muses. The tower is thereby consecrated to "his freedom, tranquility and leisure."

Following my guide up the narrow corkscrew stairs to this top floor, it amuses me to fit my feet into the same worn hollows of the stone treads that Montaigne must have trod; the apprentice footfalls literally following in the master's steps. But the attic where genius labored is a barren place. The textures of the thousand books, by his count, that once lined the room and which may have softened its hard ambiance, are missing, and the place looks like a prison, a dungeon with windows. At the age of thirty-eight, Montaigne voluntarily exiled himself from family and friends and put himself in this stone tower to serve the Muses, the cruelest and most demanding of wardens. Sometimes either Henry III or Henry of Navarre would call him out for shuttle diplomacy between their warring thrones or a turn at the Bordeaux mayoralty would be forced upon him, but this is where he spent most of his remaining twenty-one years. It's tempting to think that all those books gave him the freedom to travel through these walls, through space and time, but I've never been entirely convinced of the idea that the act of creation, of choice, grants freedom. Moreover, if freedom is to be gained, it is usually at the expense of others.

Yet, in this bastille, the human mind was liberated to discover itself, and this amazing mind put together the means for that discovery. "What do I know?" he penned one morning at his desk, and the question stimulated 103 essays in answer. The domain of human sensibility was enlarged, as Columbus's elementary navigation had recently enlarged the external world.

"But I am no longer so sanguine, being less certain than I once was as to what it is to be human," wrote Wright Morris in an essay on photography, "The Camera Eye." And it is curious that this major American novelist, so inventive of character in his pages, focused on only one human figure as a photographer: the famous back of "Uncle Harry" entering a barn door. His photographs picture the things and objects people have used: combs and chairs and implements as well as the rooms and barbershops and dining rooms they have passed through—just left, maybe. These subjects of his photographs are sympathetic companions to his fiction. Tangible possessions are transformed by Morris's wordless camera into emblems of the men and women who may have owned them, whereas the actual people could only be "captured" on the high-speed emulsion of his language. Words on paper made the real picture.

Perhaps what we mistakenly call reality is only the image that has held still long enough to be photographed. The energies and multilayered qualities of human ambition are never at rest and move too fast for ordinary film. They can only be "taken" by the novelist, the poet, or the playwright. Recent attempts to transfer to movies the wordy musings on the human condition by Wharton, James, and Conrad have resulted in earnest, entertaining failures. And we must accept the filmmakers' defense that movies are a different medium. They are. They are only composed of pictures, but are they as real as they should be? Really real?

Perhaps Montaigne's claim that he was the only subject of his essays was made once too often to believe its humility; however, looking into himself, he captured an authentic picture of his world and its citizens. Mulling through the volumes that once

lined these walls, he recovered his world's past in order to repro-
duce its present. I stand in this cool stone cell where these translations took place and still feel their heat. I think of the albums
of photographs that supposedly represent our time. Go to your
local used-magazine store and flip through the piles of old *Life*
magazines, see *Life* going to the party that was this twentieth
century. But they won't give you the whole picture. Only the
camera of the mind can produce images adequate to the authors
of the time.

"Look at that," Wright Morris will say to me in California. On
the floor beside his easy chair is a large, coffee-table format book
of photographs—the planet Earth taken from space, from the
moon. The cover shows a blue disc scarved in wispy egg whites
of clouds, and not one sign of life. "It doesn't look like anything,"
he will say.

Double
Exposure

Kodak produced the Medalist I from 1941 to 1948, and the navy adopted this sturdy camera to record some of the dire events of World War II and for that archive, which looks almost creaky in its ancient and suspended horror. The camera made a 2¼-by-3¼ negative from 620 film, focusing through a split-image range finder. The lens was first rate, an Ektar f3.5, pretty fast for its time, and the 100mm focal length permitted the photographer to frame a subject that might be more hazardous to shoot close up. Today it would be called a "portrait lens." The camera looked like a fat Leica of the M series, and it was a solid, substantial handful, for it weighed 3.25 pounds. Those of us who used it joked that if the navy suddenly transferred us to the Seabees, we could take our Medalists with us as hammers with which to build barracks and airstrips.

Reading over the above paragraph, I see I have used the past tense, which is inaccurate because a number of these cameras are still around. This includes a later model of the Medalist, the Medalist II, that Kodak put out for the civilian market that is lighter and incorporates a Flash Supermatic shutter. Clearly, flash pictures of kamikazes and beach landings would have been superfluous. Both models, in good condition, can be had today by the collector for around two hundred dollars, though the 620 film is no longer available on the market and must be obtained from a special purveyor. On more than one occasion, I've been tempted to buy one just to hold it in my hand.

This camera was first put into my hands in the early months of 1946; the hostilities were just over when I showed up at the Fleet Hometown News Center on Rush Street in Chicago. I was to be trained as a naval correspondent. The service had yet to formalize a rating for us—later "journalist mate" was used—and we had no particular symbol to wear on our left sleeves when we became petty officers. So the navy assigned us the letter X to wear above our chevrons, and this anonymous and unfamiliar classification sometimes led to amusing exchanges. Shipmates at mess who asked us what the specialist X rating stood for would be told "mortician mate" thereby guaranteeing us a near-private table.

In a workmanlike manner, we were taught on Rush Street how to estimate the light from a subject (we had no light meters), how to load film, and how to operate the camera. A former professional photographer a few months from his discharge guided us through the mysteries of the darkroom, and we paid attention because the story on him was that he had done "glamour shots" before the war of Hedy Lamar and Joan Crawford. So I acquired a working knowledge of the Medalist, how to make a picture with it, and how to develop and print that picture. How to estimate light.

I've used light meters since, and have owned several cameras with built-in light meters, but I still automatically bracket a shot as Ozzie Sweet taught me in Chicago in 1946; that is, do a couple of exposures with aperture settings on either side of the reading given me either by a hand-held light meter or one integrated into the camera itself. You can never be sure which exposure will more aptly reflect the subject—the mechanical exactness of the metered reading or the slightly off side-glance at the illumination around a subject, determined by intuition or chance. There's no exactness to be found in this matter of the right aperture, though of course an image can be captured at almost any aperture that will give an acceptable approximation, but will it be the real picture?

Trying to do the same trick with language presents a similar challenge, which may be why I admire those writers who use up a good deal of space around a subject—say, James or Faulkner or Wright Morris—trying to get the best light on the human experience in focus. They bracket their shots using different apertures of metaphor and imagery in their attempts to represent a character's sensibility at a given moment in time. All have declared, in different venues, how success will always be frustrated. The moth of truth always flits out of the frame no matter how fast the shutter speed, but as writers they must continue to qualify and qualify and qualify in an attempt to get as close to the truth as possible. The parenthetical makes some impatient, and using language skillfully is automatically suspect in certain quarters where the direct, unadorned tale is demanded by a more plebian eye. What this audience seems to expect and enjoy is a depiction that is as uncomplicated, if not as unsurprising, as a union paycheck.

We were also given some writing exercises at Fleet Hometown News Center in Chicago and made into overnight editors, processing the thousands of stories sent in from ship and shore posts for publication in newspapers around the country. Rush Street was the nucleus of the navy's public-relations effort to inform the homefolks of the importance of that service and how their sons and daughters were contributing to that importance. Our operation took up one whole floor of an office building, most of it made into what looked like the huge city room of a newspaper, complete with an immense circular copy desk. Some of us sat around this desk to edit the accounts sent in by other naval correspondents and direct them to the appropriate hometown newspapers.

> Seaman First Class Donald Winslow of Pottsville, Pennsylvania, has been enjoying the historic sites of Naples, Italy as a member of the crew of the destroyer *USS Power* that is paying a courtesy call to this famous Mediterranean port.
>
> The *Power* is accompanying the battleship *USS Missouri* on its important mission for the U.S. Naval Forces Mediterranean to support freedom in Greece.
>
> Seaman Winslow, who is working toward a Machinist Rating, expects to visit other atmospheric ports in this famous region of the world as he learns skills that will serve him for life. (Picture enclosed.)

Picture by Medalist, of course, and usually taken with the large block letters of the ship's classification in the background. Some were framed better than others, most were pretty flat in the light available, and all were posed prosaically on a ship's deck. But the sailor in each picture was definitely identifiable. Folks at home, in the neighborhood, could look at the newspaper, nod, and say, "That's Donnie all right. He's in Naples, Italy, but it looks just like him."

Now sometimes certain pictures would come across the desk that checked our routines because of the odd angle at which the Medalist must have been held or because of a curious light in the sailor's eyes—not the usual police lineup pose. The camera had caught something different, and it wasn't right. We dismissed these pictures, most of them trashed as being "arty," and we were sure the hometown newspaper editors wouldn't use them because they looked fake, not genuine. They weren't real enough.

It was great duty. We were given extra pay to feed and house ourselves because our office was in the city and too far from the barracks at the Great Lakes Naval Station, and the specialist X rating on our sleeves sparked the curiosity of jolly girls downtown from Cicero and looking for adventure. Later I was transferred to the Office of Public Relations in Washington DC, where I put my Medalist in the desk drawer and was put to composing letters and speeches for admirals, including Chester Nimitz, then the chief of naval operations.

Harry Truman was attempting to unify the armed services, so each branch hoped to prove itself unique and un-unifiable by creating legends and events through public relations that would covertly counter the president's intentions. One of our more outrageous schemes was to make the birthday of John Paul Jones into a national holiday. To this end, several of us were assigned to write a biography of the old buccaneer-turned-patriot and to flood the feature departments of newspapers with the highly colored accounts of Jones's exploits on the sea and in the boudoir. We even wrote a masque with parts to be taken by the more theatrically inclined personnel in different bases around the country. The scenes of Jones on bended knee before Catherine the Great or taking a heroic stand on the deck of the *Bon Homme Richard* are particular treasures on the shelf of my memory.

Alas, our efforts were aborted because our vigorous research also began to turn up such facts as his illegitimacy—his actual name was not Jones—and, even more startling, that the remains resting in noble peace at Annapolis might not be those of the Scots freebooter but those of some other anonymous cadaver mistakenly brought back from Paris by Teddy Roosevelt's White Fleet in 1907. So, the navy backed off.

On weekends I loaded up the Medalist to make pictures of the architectural junk pile of Washington DC, often employing these illusions or delusions as the background for the smiling appearance of a young woman. In Chicago I had discovered one way to a girl's heart could often be found through a camera lens; however, I became aware that the images of these agreeable companions had a difference from the stone façades in the background. I'm not talking about mere facial expression. Their countenances changed endlessly in the light, whereas the same light caught no shift in the marble and granite. The unpretentious face continuously evolved with every tic of thought behind it, always to escape the reality I hoped to capture with the Medalist. But my shots of the Lincoln Memorial were exact and dully correct and looked exactly like the postcards for sale in every drugstore. As I was to learn later, "Objects have a sense of their own, a mystic meaning proper to themselves to give out." I was too naïve, too ignorant, to receive their meaning. I just wasn't getting it. I am to learn that the sensibility of the picture taker must be part of the picture taken, and it is true, I think, of writing as well.

Meanwhile, the navy had decided on a stunt guaranteed to get headlines and prove its uniqueness. At the end of the war, American troops had captured the v-2 rocket facilities from which the Germans launched these terrifying weapons across the Channel on a hapless English population. Van Braun and his associates had happily surrendered to American authorities with every expectation of a new citizenship, and they were not disappointed. These huge rockets were transported to White Sands, New Mexico, for testing, where their feckless instability was quickly discovered. Some merely blew up on the launch pad; others would rise a hundred feet, pause, and then tiredly fall to earth—everyone running for cover. Still others would lift off, then tip over, and race across the desert floor at eight hundred miles per hour before encountering a cactus or a rock outcropping and exploding.

"No one has ever launched one off a moving ship."

My informant is Captain E. B. Dexter, deputy director of navy public relations. It is a sweltering August day, and I have been called over from another bureau where I have been editing a news service sent out to ship and shore newspapers. Captain Dexter is a handsome man, a graduate of Annapolis, and only thirty-eight, which means that flag rank could come to him at an unusually early age. He is brilliant, cool as we say today, and he has held his deadpan as long as he could. "This is a top secret operation, Masters. You are not to tell anyone about this assignment. That's an order."

He goes on to say that the navy has decided to launch two of these rockets from the deck of the USS *Midway*, the largest of the Navy's carriers and, it would be my guess, the largest ship afloat at that time. My assignment is to help him with the different media outlets to publicize this historic moment. I am to write stories and take pictures of the key personnel in the launch, and I'm also to interview these men with a wire recorder for broadcast on the Mutual Radio Network. In addition, I'm to prepare a dummy story with blanks to be filled in with the names of the ship's company—several thousand names—all to be processed by the Fleet Hometown News Center and released to the newspapers after the successful completion of Operation Sandy. The occasion has been so named.

As I say, this event took place in August of 1947. A couple of months earlier, Wright Morris had set up his four-by-five Graphic View camera on a tripod in Norfolk, Nebraska, to take pictures of objects he remembered from his youth on the family farm. Here I must identify that earlier quote as a speculation phrased by Henry James in *The American Scene* and which Morris uses as an epigraph for his 1948 photo-text novel, *The Home Place*. This book has been reissued by the University of Nebraska Press with a fine introduction by John Hollander. It is a unique volume that combines narrative text with eighty-nine photographs, the same ones Morris made just before I was assigned to Operation Sandy, and some others made a year or two earlier. These photographs were not to illustrate the immediate text but to provide a sort of mutual "seeing" of the rooms the novel inhabits and the objects its characters handle, sit in, look at.

Morris's boxy Graphic was a little more complicated than my Medalist in that the lens board could be moved to rise and fall to correct for parallax distortion in addition to the usual "back and forth" positioning for perspective and focus. He had used a smaller version of this camera with a Schneider Angulon lens, and he might have transferred or used the same lens to the larger camera. I can find no exact information on this point. Both cameras used film cut and arranged in square packs that could be removed and reinserted in the back of the box. The image was focused on a ground-glass screen. The photographer composed and focused the image while hunched under a black hood, the camera on a tripod, and, as in the classic projection of the original *camera*, what he saw would be upside down.

Not a rig for taking snapshots; however, the Graflex Company also produced the famous Speed Graphic camera, a cousin to the camera Morris used. This square so-called press camera of mid-century—often with a flash-bulb unit fixed to its left side—also took some of the more memorable images of World War II. It weighed in at around five pounds, focused with a range finder, and was a standard prop in movies of the period with scenarios that included newspapermen or the subject of celebrity. But I have strayed from Wright Morris the novelist hunched under a black cloth in Norfolk, Nebraska.

Of the eighty-nine photographs in *The Home Place*, only four portray a human figure, and in none of these can Uncle Harry's face be seen. He's either turned away from the camera, or the light from his face has been overexposed, the aperture opened up, so his straw hat floats over a black space. In the final picture of the novel, on the last page as well, the old farmer steps into the black vault of a barn's interior—perhaps into what the ancients called the doorway into darkness. All four photographs of him hint that if you want to see what Uncle Harry looks like, what he's *really* like, then you must read the narrative, where he is "seen" talking and walking, lighting his pipe, or making heart-stopping gestures such as fishing a dime from the front pocket of his bib overalls. Meanwhile, Morris, as the photographer, has found and focused on the mystic meaning in this human object that has been worn and handled by a life of toil on the prairie. "One of the few (relics) that still almost worked," to quote Morris from *Photographs and Word*. Uncle Harry has been put into the same drawer with the homely tableware on page 39, washed up and neatly arrayed on the page of a newspaper used to line the drawer. The round tops of three of the blades partially obscure a picture in the newspaper that is identified as "Hitler's Army Chief" to make a visual digression that is a small masterpiece all its own.

I read *The Home Place* as one of those quizzical arguments Morris often made in his novels and essays, and I can see that questioning side-look come into his eye. Here, perhaps, the subject is the ultimate failure of language to represent an accurate picture of human experience—the site of that experience—alongside the inability of photographs to do the job alone without words. As writers we are all participants who must report the matter—to further paraphrase James's suggestion—and some of us attempt to minimize this inherent failure of the enterprise by playing with the lighting and making several shots of the subject. Others seem satisfied with a more modest record, convinced of its genuineness by its simplicity. Both may be fake and neither very real.

What the navy is attempting to do in 1947 with Operation Sandy is to seize the imagination of the public by an illustration of its expertise with these huge rockets people had only become aware of. In 1947 we are twenty-two years from landing on the moon, but that landing had been imagined for centuries, and the desire to travel through space must have come with the first glance at a star. Some beings may have a general understanding about gravity, but only humans have plotted to escape its grasp, and that desire coupled with dreaming creates a need not all that different from what some of us feel in writing—to break the earth-bound nature of language. As Goethe said, "We are drawn to stars that want us not."

In Norfolk, Virginia, where I board the *Midway*, the top-secret nature of Operation Sandy was discussed in every bar on Granby Street. My mother seems to be the only person who doesn't know what my assignment is about. Sworn to secrecy by Captain Dexter, I have refused her information when I phoned to ask that my white uniforms be airmailed back from Philadelphia, where she was having them laundered. What a delicious moment Captain Dexter has unknowingly granted me—to deny information to my mother! A new authority had replaced the old, and I happily enlisted in my new fealty. I was to learn later that she had even phoned the office of Admiral Nimitz, demanding to know where I had been sent and why. She was told nothing.

So I climb the steep gangplank up and into the huge mass of the *Midway*, free of old obligations, with my sea bag, my Medalist, and the heavy and cumbersome wire recorder—certain that I am about to become part of a historic occasion. These early recording devices weighed about forty pounds—we're still in the vacuum-tube period, and most of the weight was due to heavy batteries. Sound is recorded on a magnetized wire on two spools and passes through the recording heads. The wire is only a little thicker than a human hair and often breaks and has to be mended by tying the ends into a square knot and welding this tiny hitch with the glowing tip of a cigarette.

I am billeted with some marines who have accompanied the missiles from White Sands, New Mexico, and who are to be posted as Operation Sandy's own security guards. No officer or crewman of the *Midway*, not even the carrier's own detachment of marines, are allowed anywhere near the rockets. It's all top secret. As we get underway, my bunkmates tell me scary stories about how the v-2s had exploded or gone astray in the desert, and as far as they were concerned, Operation Sandy was only one more demonstration of the navy's dumbness. But their talk sounds to me like the usual marine grouse with the navy. Our quarters are in the forward section of the bow and seem to be surrounded by gun replacements continually practicing. The banging of the five-inch .38s is deafening and constant, for the *Midway* is maintaining battle readiness throughout. Hellcats and Avengers take off and practice landings around the clock.

On the hangar deck below, the yellow button on my jumper admits me to an area at the aft end of the ship enclosed by a high tarpaulin wall. Here are the rockets and their fuel. I have seen the v-2s in newsreels lifting off from their bases in Belgium—these pictures made by the Germans for their own newsreels—and close up they look like ugly, giant toys on their dollies. Clearly they have no other purpose but destruction. There are three of them: one painted yellow and the other two decorated with bands of red, white, and black. The pointed noses are red. They are about fifty feet long, five feet in diameter at the center, and twelve feet across the rear fins. Nearby are two immense spherical tanks painted bright orange and several squarish ones of a dull gray. Navy gray. The orange tanks are stenciled "Liquid Oxygen," and the gray ones hold a mixture of ethyl alcohol and water. The smoking lamps are out in the area.

I begin my assignment and interview an officer in charge of the area. He tells me, and the wire recorder, that the v-2's rocket engine burns a mixture of the liquid oxygen and the alcohol compound. Yes, sometimes there are failures. Bearings in the fuel line can become frozen or the feed system, powered by hydrogen peroxide steam generators, will just quit. The rocket has to go straight up; any deviation one way or another will improperly mix the fuel. The Germans, he tells me, had as many as five failures a night—clearly never seen in their newsreels—saving London from even more devastation. And they had had some problems in New Mexico, too.

"What do I mean about problems?" He repeats my question, and I have turned off the wire recorder, pretty sure the answer will not be right for the Mutual Network. "Sometimes it just sits there. Or it goes off at a crazy angle. In the desert, not many problems to it."

"But here?"

He looks at the orange tanks nearby. "Throw away your Ronson. We got the hottest lighter fluid there is right here."

I take his picture, making several exposures.

I can see Wright setting up his tripod in the kitchen of the farmhouse in Norfolk, Nebraska, and focusing the Schneider Angulon lens of his Graphic on the Home Comfort range. It burned both coal and corn cobs. He would compose the picture carefully. The square stove sits substantially on the linoleum-covered floor just next to the slim strip of an open doorway. The next room could be a parlor or a bedroom. The nickel chrome trim of the stove is clean and untarnished, and a round cast-aluminum teakettle sits on the cooking surface. Above are two rectangular warming ovens, also with doors trimmed in nickel chrome, and just over these, on a shelf, sits what looks to be a Granger tobacco tin—maybe for conserving cooking fat—and to the left, the small square shape of a French box of seasoning, maybe pepper. From the cooking surface, and through all of the above, rises the black tin trunk of the chimney.

To the left of the stove is the portion of a table that bears what looks like a stainless-steel canister, possibly for sugar or salt, and a box of Super Suds and a bottle that might contain vinegar. Go back to the French box of seasoning on the top shelf. The lettering cannot be read because the print is too fine, so I can only guess its contents—pepper or nutmeg or cinnamon. I identify it as some kind of seasoning because of the familiar black flag on the box that is the French company's trademark.

But the fact that the lettering on the box cannot be read suggests that Wright had to open up the aperture wide to take in the light available in the kitchen at that moment, which shortened the depth of focus of the lens—even using a tripod and a slow speed. Shutter speed and lens aperture observe a sibling relationship determined by the light refracted from the object and the object's mobility. This stove is not going anywhere on its own, so I am guessing that Wright made several adjustments—qualifications, if you will—of the existing light from the object by changing aperture and shutter speed to get the picture that appears on page 26 of *The Home Place*. The real picture of the Home Comfort range.

It's likely that in one of the other exposures he made of the stove, the fine print on the French box can be made out, that the kind of seasoning can be discerned, but I'm convinced that the print from that negative would not have the snap of truth as does the one printed in *The Home Place*. The chrome would be dulled or the teakettle would not be so defined, and the black stovepipe might have disappeared altogether into the rear recess of the stove. In his manipulations of shutter speed and aperture, Wright has captured the mystic meaning of the Home Comfort range—it is still warm and the coals are about to be poked up to fry some eggs. You can smell the sinus-shriveling heat it throws off. It is real.

Reading over the above, I see that I have slipped into the familiar. My friend and mentor, Winfield Townley Scott, introduced me to Wright Morris's novels in the 1950s. *My Uncle Dudley, Man and Boy, Works of Love,* and *Field of Vision* were the books the poet had recommended to me. I read them and most of the large oeuvre that followed these novels, so when Ted Weiss introduced us in the 1970s, I was already familiar with the sound of that bemused sensibility as it separated and pondered the perplexities of the human heart—separated and then rewove them into the fiber of our common pull. I knew the little orphan boy in *Works of Love*. He was I. Wright had been exiled from his native Nebraska at fifteen, as I had been pulled at fourteen from the neighborhood that had nurtured me in Kansas City. Both locales became the same territory we tried to get back to the rest of our lives.

But sitting in Ted and Renee's living room in Princeton, where Wright was a visiting writer, I became tongue-tied, a nervous post, though at the time I had published three novels and some stories. What some may see as conceit in that last statement is really only an effort to place the relationship within a timeframe—a poor means perhaps, and one more demonstration of the failure of language, at least within some intellects. Josephine Morris's voice was quite different from Wright's whiskered flatness, but it completely complimented him as she did in life. She was an early champion of the work of Dibenkorn and Motherwell and had established an important art gallery on the West Coast. Her energetic, forthright opinions were made with a clarion directness—no nonsense or misunderstandings allowed. She was impressive and inspired trust immediately. But I am digressing.

The quiet irony in Wright's talk slipped over my dazed cognizance—I was missing most of his jokes, and only recognized something humorous had transpired afterward by the oblique signals that flickered in his eyes or the pursed wryness of his mouth. Later I would see something of Eddie Cahow in his manner. Cahow is the town barber of Central City, Nebraska—Wright's actual hometown and a few miles south of Norfolk—and *The Home Place* has five pictures of Cahow's barbershop: four interior and one of the striped pole outside on the sidewalk. These constitute the most pictures of a single site in the book except for the different rooms of the farmhouse in Norfolk, which Wright made a couple of years earlier with the smaller 3¼ x 4¼ Graphic View. So this interior and its objects—the shop had formerly been a local bank—must have held a special mystique for him. It is the setting for a wonderfully comic series of scenes in the novel's narrative; a graceful meld of the two actual visits Wright made of this home place into a single return of his character in the book.

Eddie Cahow's barbershop is a place of locution and elocution, of wisecracks and verbal invention on the spot between barber and customer or another client waiting his turn in the chair. There is only one chair, another having been broken by kids excessively pumping its handle as they waited to be clipped. The wit of the talk in the photographs waits in the shaving mug, and it is lined up with the tonics and lotions ordered on the top of the oak cabinet. It is reflected in the large mirror hanging above this furniture. The talk is in the air. The painted column outside marked this outpost, perhaps the last outpost of easy male banter unhindered by the female. I can see Wright in the place, taking up a straight razor to hone it on the leather strap hanging from the chair or meticulously arranging the several hair brushes on the clean white napkin, and all the while delivering some offhand consideration of the past, the use of memory, the elusive quality of the present. "Well, for Gosh's sake," he'd say with that odd scrape of a laugh, "do you remember what Augustine said about all this?"

Several cards have been stuck into the mirror's frame, possibly from customers who have left Central City, and that possibility relates to the magic of these pictures—of all of them in the book—because these empty interiors are peopled. These rooms are "forever occupied," his narrator says in *The Home Place*, "with the people gone, you know the place is inhabited. There's something in the rooms, in the air that raising the windows won't let out. There's a pattern on the wall where the calendar's hung and the tipped square of a missing picture is a lidded eye on something private, something better not seen."

Wright's eye, his looking into an object's meaning, caught the Home Comfort stove's uniqueness at that point in time. It sits on the linoleum-covered floor of that kitchen in Norfolk, Nebraska, like no other stove, as no other stove could in a kind of elitism of its being. Others might picture the stove more equitably, see it as one of many such stoves, and so be blinded to the intrinsic nature of it by some prosaic ideology.

There is very little mystic meaning to be found in the tall yellow object that has been guyed to the rear edge of the flight deck on the USS *Midway*. It would be a far reach to compare it to the GANO grain elevator that Wright made a picture of in 1940, even though he describes the blinding white granary as looking like a rocket about to roar from the prairie. But there is not a snag on the v-2's sleekness on which to catch a gist of anything other than destruction. This dummy rocket has been mounted and wired down between a pair of frameworks that are hinged to the deck so that they can fall away with a tremendous crash to leave the v-2 standing on its four fins. These supports are of tubular steel, and the whole rig resembles the Tinkertoy construction of a gigantic, demented child.

I take pictures of this apparatus with the Medalist from the fore end of the deck, some nine hundred feet away, putting this splinter into focus, this sliver of fantasy sticking straight up in the brilliant Caribbean sunlight. It doesn't belong there on the aft deck of the *Midway*, but there it is in my viewfinder, and as enthusiastic as I have been for the navy's mission, I am very aware of the slight heave and roll of the deck beneath my feet. "No one has ever launched one from a moving ship," Captain Dexter had said.

"These babies get up to eight hundred miles per hour in just four seconds after they start to burn. Then they go sonic." He's a chief gunner's mate in charge of this part of the launch. "It wouldn't be practical to tie them down. So once ignition starts, we drop these support frames. That's what we're practicing now."

"So once this framework drops away, it will just stand on its fins? By itself?"

I hold the microphone close to his face, but he doesn't answer immediately. He's looking out over the flat plain of the sea. A sort of merry look comes into his eyes. "That's right," he says at last. "We never had trouble before. Of course, we've never done this before—on a moving ship, I mean."

After evening chow, I locate an ensign who is responsible for the fueling of the rocket. He's wearing crisp suntans and still has the fuzz of NROTC on his cheeks. "Each rocket contains 10,800 pounds of liquid oxygen; 8,400 pounds of fuel mix . . ."

"That's the alcohol and water?"

". . . That's right. Then about 400 pounds of hydrogen peroxide to fuel the turbo pump. The whole rig weighs in at about 28,500 pounds—the rocket itself being about 9,000 pounds." He is proud of these figures.

"It must be risky fuelling the rocket."

"Not very." He's nonchalant and just a little bored by the question. "The tricky part is once it starts burning. It has to burn straight up. If the rocket tips one way or another, the fuel proportion gets compromised and then we're in trouble."

We are standing next to the two red, white, and black rockets, looking scary on their carriages. The tanks of liquid oxygen and fuel are around us and just beneath what will be the launch pad on the flight deck above. There, the steel framework has crashed down to the deck in another jarring practice run.

The routine of shipboard life continues. The *Midway* stays its course, and sailors sunbathe on the fore flight deck. No planes are landing now. The boatswain's shrill whistle precedes garbled announcements over the intercom. Several basketball games are played in the part of the hangar deck that has not been curtained off. But this ordinary domain with its own clock determining the different stations runs concurrently and in conflict with the preparations for Operation Sandy. The rig on the aft end of the flight deck falls in a monotonous cacophony. The technicians that accompanied the rockets from New Mexico attend to their different tasks. It is an odd combination of the normal and the abnormal, all making way through the sea on the 45,000 tons of floating steel called the USS *Midway*.

Several decks below in the ship's bowels, I talk with a chief electronics mate in a compact compartment guarded by a couple of my marine bunkmates. They are heavily armed. Several panels of electronic boards take up one wall of the compartment—large dials and switches, an array of colored lights. It resembles a very complicated pinball machine on end. A small package of electronic sensors has been packed into the nose of each rocket, and this equipment is to send back signals from the rocket in flight to this command post. In the small remaining space, several men practice a pattern of movement that resembles a razzle-dazzle backfield play. They shout commands to each other in German. These are some of the technicians who had originally created the v-2 and who now work for the United States and its guided missile program. It's been rumored that Van Braun himself is on board.

"What do I think of this?" the chief answers my question. "I'm going on my third hitch in the navy. I've worked hard and learned my rate and look where I am. I'm with a bunch of machines that are smarter than me and a bunch of Krauts I can't understand. Here's what I do in this Operation Sandy. I push this button right here. I won't even get to see the damn thing fly off. What will I tell my kids when they ask me what I did? Can I tell them I pushed this button? They do that every Halloween."

I managed to save some of that interview after careful editing.

In his introduction to a new edition of *The Home Place*, John Hollander says that the novel was written after the pictures were taken. The emulsion of the two forms is so smooth, so effortlessly mixed, that the whole book "reads" as if it came together all in one. But of course it didn't. Wright had received a second Guggenheim and returned to Norfolk with the larger camera to make the pictures of the farm and Uncle Harry. I can imagine him looking over the resulting prints, judging them for their accuracy, but thanks to Hollander's information, I can wonder at the point of his inspection when he chose not to collect the images into another anthology of photographs. A few years earlier Walker Evans had published his *Let Us Now Praise Famous Men*, with accompanying text by James Agee. I wonder if the enigmatic figure of Uncle Harry became a sort of cicerone that led the writer's eye into a narrative that would neither explain nor illustrate the pictures but would reflect on the mystical meaning of the pictures as the pictures themselves did similarly of their subjects. It would be a double-mirror perspective that might occur in Eddie Cahow's barber chair, holding a hand mirror to the back of the head while looking straight ahead into the larger mirror on the wall.

"What's this old man doing?" is the question asked in the first line of the novel, and the answer transforms the old farmer from icon into a narrative device as he ambles through the story, commenting and correcting, causing a crisis in the plotline here and there. As I say, his photograph appears four times, but he has surely just passed through the other photographs—he occupies the rooms of that farmhouse. Uncle Harry is a walking negative capability. I better say no more, for I can see that cool laughter coiling in Wright's eyes, ready to strike down my presumption.

One time during a symposium sponsored by the University of Nebraska, a panelist read a very long paper about some flies trapped between the screen and window in the novel *Ceremony at Lone Tree*. The theory went on and on. The image was a symbol of the novel's characters being trapped in the frames of their existence. Wasn't the whole window unit a symbol of the human predicament, to be confined and destined to die within the luminous structure of our own cognizance? Something like that. The acetylene burned bright in Wright's eyes as he got up to dryly respond that, yes, the flies in that window were pretty dead all right, and as far as symbols went, he thought the whole novel was a symbol.

His friendship of a quarter of a century helped define my perception of myself as a writer and photographer. His work gave me confidence to see a place and its inhabitants through language and that the bare minutes of that meeting are not enough. His correspondence was sprightly and often droll, and sometimes he signed his letters, Uncle Dudley—the character in his first novel who takes his nephew on a transcontinental odyssey in a Marmon touring sedan. Later, there would be phone calls ("I can no longer write, Hilary"), the dry whisk of voice coming at the subject from the side, and I learned to anticipate some play of language to invigorate the idea with a splash of fun, a tonic familiar to Eddie Cahow's barbershop.

But we are deadly serious in August of 1947, and the weighty significance of our mission has been made heavier by the number of high-ranking brass that have hopped off a helicopter onto the flight deck. Generals of the army and the marines, admirals of different stars have just been flown over from Bermuda. The green hulk of the island has mysteriously materialized in the morning light. Among them is the slim, dapper figure of Admiral William H. P. Blandy, head of the navy's guided missile program. He wears suntans, the shirt open at the throat, and the large-billed cap made popular by William Halsey. He moves with a lithe grace and has a long beak of a nose—all of which propel the ship rumor that he was part Apache. So much for the romance of men at sea.

A voice over the PA that evening clearly defined what we were up too. "This is Sandy minus twenty-eight." Twenty-eight hours before liftoff, and the hours would be counted off, then the minutes of the last hour, and then the seconds of the final minute—just like the movies—before this historic occasion when civilization, thanks to the U.S. Navy, would make a grab for the stars.

That night I lugged the wire recorder up to Captain Dexter's stateroom. He had been on board from the beginning, and we had already met several times to prepare the different parts of the press coverage. We have supervised the installation of motion picture cameras, bolted to the deck, that would film the event for Movietone News. The cameras were to operate remotely because, for safety precautions, no crewmember was to be allowed above deck save for ship's crew trained to handle the flaming wreckage of a crashed plane. I have pictures of them crouched behind and around the carrier's command island.

After I set up the wire recorder, Captain Dexter reads into the microphone a short statement he has prepared, briefly recounting the rocket's history and the navy's bold reasons for launching a couple from a moving ship. Oddly, I can't remember what those were. His talk is in the present tense and, as we rehearsed, I switch off the recorder as he says, "And the next sound you will hear will be the mighty roar of the V-2 rocket's engines as it lifts from the deck of the *Midway* on its historic flight." I count one-two-three and flip the switch, praying the thin wire would not buckle and snap. It doesn't. We looked at each other and Captain Dexter gives a funny laugh.

"This is Sandy minus six." The yellow dummy has been replaced by the real thing. The three colors of the painted bands make the V-2 both comical and ominous. I have no doubt one of them must stand at the entrance of some amusement park today, but that morning, the sea very calm, it was damn frightening. I realize the only way to get it off the ship now—it was fully fueled—is to shoot it off. "This is Sandy minus two."

Wright and others have taught me to see the end of a scene and, once seen, to get off the stage quickly, so I'm trying to compress this action. I wish I could say I found some mystical meaning in the object that stood straight up between its metal supports on the end of the *Midway*'s flight deck, but even as a detached and interested participant—to rearrange James's conceit a little—I could only think of those Fourths of July on Roberts Street in Kansas City, when we would send tin cans high into the elms above with the blast of two-inch firecrackers. Some of us labor to raise such ordinary acts into metaphor and burning polemics that all too often fall back into sentimentality—mawkish disasters. To transform the commonplace, the human place, into a meaning that is both natural and exalted takes a special eye such as the one that looked at the Home Comfort stove in Norfolk, Nebraska.

During this digression, the countdown has gotten to the last minute and is reckoning by seconds: "45—44—43—42—." All the brass, Captain Dexter, and I are crammed into the snug flight bridge halfway up the control island on the starboard center of the carrier. I am the only noncom and Captain Dexter is the only officer without a star on his collar. Admiral Blandy is at the front of the group and leans over the waist-high railing to look aft. The long bill of his cap and the point of his aquiline nose seem to direct everyone's attention to the macabre apparatus at the end of the flight deck. "29—28—27—26." The *Midway* barely creeps through the flat sea, just making steerage speed, but it has to be said—it is moving. I have placed the wire recorder on a chart table, warmed it up. Everything looks okay—no crimp in the wire. Since I am the last in the pack, I must rise on tiptoe to see over the shoulders of the generals and admirals to view the missile. I think of the different men I have talked to, all of them waiting to push the different buttons assigned to them. I pray the delicate wire will not jam or break. "9—8—7—6." Almost there.

One of the officers says, "Damn," as if to relieve his own tension. "3—2—1—blast off." I touch the record lever and press it down at Captain Dexter's nod. The spools turn smoothly, and I hold the microphone up and over the heads of the officers. But nothing is happening. An eerie stillness encloses the *Midway*.

Then a wee whistle is heard that increases rapidly in depth and volume, and flame shoots out from beneath the rocket to curl around its fins. The framework still embraces it. The noise has become deafening. Every IRT train in Manhattan is coming down the same track, and the steel plates beneath our feet begin to vibrate. The framework is still in place, and I am counting. Surely four seconds have elapsed. Then, with a crash, the steel harness drops to the deck, but the rocket stays balanced on its four fins. A tiny flame has just spilled from between a couple of the rocket's panels halfway up its girth. This isn't supposed to happen. The volume meter on the wire recorder is jammed against the dial. Admiral Blandy's face has hardened, but he continues to stare down at the rocket. He seems to have willed it to get off the deck, for it has slowly begun to rise into the air—slowly and with great effort—and then it's scarlet nose tips forward. It points straight at us. It seems to pause, and then with a great roar and whoosh it flies over us, missing the radar antenna by about ten feet.

"Where the hell did it go," shouts Captain Dexter, and all of us rush to the other side of the platform, to the starboard side of the ship, which now gives me a front-row seat. We watch its drunken flight until about six miles away it straightens up, begins to climb, and blows up. Ka-POW! The fuel mixture has been thrown off, I tell myself. Pieces of metal fleck the sea and fall on one of the escort destroyers that have accompanied us to keep nosey Soviet subs at a distance.

The demonstration has impressed one of the generals. "When do we launch the next one, Admiral?"

Blandy regards the man steadily for a little and then says, "When I get off this fucking tub."

So, we return to Norfolk. The newsreels show the rocket rising from the deck, and the radio broadcasts Captain Dexter's eye-witness account—his final inquiry and Blandy's response to the general erased—and thousands of hometown newspapers learn that their sons have been part of a historic moment. The navy got is headlines.

The pictures I made with the Medalist might still be in some navy archive, but the recorded interviews and the feature stories have surely disappeared into the dustbin. Wright Morris died in 1998. He left behind novels, short stories, essays, and the photographs he made in Nebraska and other places—even Venice. He left them behind as he passed through this habitat we share, this history and landscape; words and pictures that occupy the rooms of our being, generating their own light.

Silence, Please

Some claim that community is founded in conversation, and it is true that the slightest exchange establishes a common ground. These fellowships, however transient, may originate even as we ask directions in a strange part of town or share an opinion on the weather, but I have also followed long stretches of silence on the back roads of France and Italy and felt refreshed by the lack of gab. As the kilometers turned on the odometer, I have gone a whole day without speaking and have often played with the fancy that the facility for speech had left me. When I stopped for a night's lodging, I might have to employ sign language. With or without bath? I would stand dumbly before the question.

To travel in a foreign land, where one is not all that easy with the language spoken, imposes a solitude that some find unacceptable, even frightening. The isolation oppresses them, and they are stung by the sense that they draw breath in a surrounding that gets along without their input. The more philosophical may hear the ominous soundings of the ultimate alienation that awaits us all. But I embrace this recess from language and enjoy its curious freedom.

Speaking up is an attribute we supposedly admire; we claim

to esteem the outspoken personality. "He says what he thinks," is an assessment given as praise though the value of the thought is sometimes questionable. These days our common airwaves are saturated with the gabble of so-called authorities, talking all at once, and this rude furor is meant to simulate intellectual discussion. The racket makes no sense, nor is it meant to do so, for our time has become impatient with content.

I can give no inventory of the thoughts that ran silently and probably not all that deeply through my mind as I followed Route DI south on a beautiful day in the Meuse Valley. If I refer to my journal kept during that tour, I will find only fragmentary accounts: details of landscape and food eaten, the aspect of a village, a historical site noted. But the thoughts that kept me company during that solitary junket have disappeared like the breezes that wafted through the car's windows. I hope they may have lodged in the walls of my imagination, my soul, as the Ancients used that word.

The verbal exchanges in the family life I saw on the screen of the Chief Theatre in Kansas City were a beguiling enigma, foreign to my experience. How could people talk so much at the dinner table, so pleasantly trade comments? Where did all those words come from, and where did they get that material? My grandparents' dinner table was a silent business, each of them covertly waiting for the other to say something that could be contradicted or ridiculed. So it was a standoff, and we ate in silence. Later, my grandfather's eloquence would enfold me in his bedroom, away from my grandmother's ironic asides, as he told me stories of his early years. Her speech, melodious as it was profoundly idiomatic, was preserved for teatime confabs with cousins or sisters or in those moments when she would rise to address a convention as the innocent spokesperson for the squalid Pendergast political machine.

But when my mother appeared in this still life, the noise of her upset us. She smashed our mute decorum with rowdy narratives of her life in New York City that turned the dinner table into a sounding board for opinions and pronouncements that none of us could process. She stunned us. I know now that much of what she said was a boisterous quilt she pieced together to cover the solitude of her life with, and then without, my father.

Visiting my parents in New York, I would stand entranced before the representation of Neanderthal family life in the Museum of Natural History. As adult males sharpened stone spearheads, females tended supper, cooking over an open fire while children played with beads and small stones. All silent behind the glass. The staged harmony of these manikins was familiar to me; I recognized their wordless cohabitation.

Families this side of the glass pursue their daily routines similarly. I know of one that went about its address with a purposeful restraint. Disagreeable matters were swept under the rug and crises, if acknowledged, were appeased rather than met. "I don't want to hear about it," was the cry in response to a difficulty. The children acquired an aptitude for the tacit, stepping tight-lipped through rooms of small talk. In their own maturity, they turned this honed reserve upon their elders as if to punish them for the expertise they had learned from them.

Thoreau, our national icon of aloneness, claimed "the truest society approaches always nearer to solitude," but Henry was also known to leave his lakeside retreat and go home to his mother's for supper. So asking for the gravy to be passed had not completely lost importance, and even he would have to admit that in the absence of civil exchange, anarchy masquerades as freedom. Yet our genius has enabled us to magnify our words into the realms of prattle, and the resulting clamor imprisons us. Language is no longer a component of order, as academic jargon competes with political euphemisms to make a solecistic din that deafens the essential dialogues. Have we been brought all this way, Stephen Crane might ask, to drown in our own gibberish?

Disorderly
Conduct

In jail in Worcester. It is February 1978, one week after the huge blizzard that has imprisoned all of New England, and I have just been locked up in a basement cell of the old police department on Waldo Street in Worcester, Massachusetts.

"What time is it? Does anyone know what time it is?"

The cry comes from a prisoner several cells to my right. I cannot see him. It must be about one in the morning, February 17. My son's birthday. A few hours from now, and about 120 miles west of here, his mother will wake him. "Happy birthday, honey," she will say. "How's it feel to be a teenager?" He is thirteen years old. But I don't know what time it is because my wristwatch, along with my other valuables, has been deposited with the police clerk. A raw bruise made by the handcuff encircles my left wrist, where my watch should be. It took three cops almost five minutes to undo the bracelet when I was being booked. The arresting officer had fastened the handcuff.

"That's a little tight, isn't it?" I had said. The cop had pushed me facedown over the hood of his squad car to hook my hands behind my back. The night was very cold, and we are standing in a small arroyo of piled snow.

"I can make it tighter," he replied and squeezed up another notch on the cuff to prove it.

"What is this about?" I asked him. He looks very young, and he is shivering though he had just jumped out of the heated cruiser. So he's not all that cold. His partner, who drove the cruiser, is calm but sarcastic. "We do things differently here than in New York." He had checked my driver's license by flashlight. It is around eleven o'clock and there is no one on the street. This corner of Worcester is like some remote part of the Yukon—still and frozen.

The '60s have educated me as to how a badge can be worn by the wrong person. Nightsticks wielded lawlessly in the hands of the law. Selma. Greensboro. Chicago. I am thinking that there are no witnesses here on Main Street in Worcester. I had put up resistance, the cops could say later, and they had to use force to subdue me. They had not meant to kill me, but I had kept resisting arrest. These things happen. I kept asking questions, so I was a wise guy. I had asked them for their names. Quinn and Germain. Quinn had cuffed me and, in doing so, became the designated arresting officer. He's only been on the street, it turns out, four months.

"Sometimes," my grandfather used to tell me, "they'd let a fellow go. Unlock the cell and say, 'Vamoose,' and the galoot would get to the door of the calaboose and they'd shoot him in the back. Say he was trying to escape." But that was in Mexico and in the time of Porfirio Diaz. This is Worcester, Massachusetts, in 1978, and I am terrified.

"What's going on?" I asked again. The hood of the police cruiser warms one side of my face. "What's this about?"

"Disturbing the peace," Officer Quinn replied and pulled me up and turned me around. They have called the paddy wagon to take me to jail.

Prison has been the ideal study for many writers; great literature has been created behind bars. At one o'clock in the morning I am calling their roll in order to take my place beside them. Cervantes, Raleigh, Dostoevsky, Thoreau, O. Henry. Let's not forget de Sade and Genet. How about Mailer? Even Mailer was thrown in the clink. Jail is not such a bad life for a writer. All that I require is some paper and a pencil, and I can keep going. I don't need a seat on the toilet. I don't need shoe laces or a belt to hold up my pants. Just pass me paper and a pencil through the bars along with the prison grub. Besides, I'm out of the weather; it's below zero outside. As for loss of liberty, a special freedom exists within enclosure. Restraint releases one from responsibility, from those duties imposed by the social contract and the burden of normal relationships—even from a marriage going sour.

I should appreciate the irony of my arrest and embrace the opportunity of my imprisonment. Perhaps here in the privacy of my cell in the basement of this old building, I can finish the manuscript I have been lugging around the country for the last several years. I think of those happy monks of Clonmacnois, on the banks of the River Shannon, warmly cloistered and doodling, penning one illumination upon another to ignite the gloomy keep of their convictions. The family memoir I started three years ago in New York City, before driving west to Iowa to teach at Drake University, is almost finished. I have come to Worcester to teach at Clark University and have wound up in jail. And what's the difference? Isn't this stone cube with steel bars, with its marble slab for a bed, the ultimate retreat I have been seeking all these years—the pension I had thought to locate in academia? Moreover, here I will be given an identification, a number on my back, which might satisfy my wife's growing uncertainty as to who I am. "What is it you do?" my brother-in-law keeps asking. I have claimed to be a writer; yet my third novel was published seven years ago and despite the valiant efforts of my agent, nothing else has appeared in print. So to acquire some kind of identity, if not a little income, I have accepted invitations to teach, to be a visiting writer on campus.

But now I am just one more transient in this old lockup on Waldo Street in Worcester, Massachusetts. The building was designed by George H. Clemence, a local architect, and completed in 1918. His design is a compact example of the Renaissance Revival popular at that time. The four-storied pressed-brick façade is ornately trimmed in terracotta with rondelles and foliated windows; so, by day, the building resembles a wing of the Uffizi that has somehow been detached and relocated in this old industrial city in central Massachusetts. The basement jail is saturated with authentic Renaissance odors.

But this is the middle of the night, so I cannot appreciate Clemence's genius from this low vantage point. Nor had it been my choice to visit this landmark in the first place! "Enjoy the trip, Professor," Officer Germain had said as I was lifted up the rear steps of the paddy wagon. Had Holy Cross been my host institution, the officer's attitude toward me might have been different. "What are you doing in Worcester?" Officer Germain had asked, looking at my New York driver's license. He had ignored the rest of the identification I offered him, brushed it aside; membership cards in the Authors Guild and the American Society of Magazine Photographers. These cops are like my brother-in-law.

"I am a visiting faculty member at Clark University." The campus is within walking distance.

"Where are you going and where are you coming from?" the younger cop asked.

"I'm going home. My apartment is just around the corner. I'm coming from a party near the campus."

"Have you been drinking, Professor?"

Two drinks. The party had broken up early. I have answered calmly, aware of the sarcasm growing in their address. *Professor.* I put my mind onto something else. I had been doing research yesterday in the Clark Library on James Audubon. His wife's name was Germaine. With an *e*. Briefly, I fooled with the idea that Officer Germain might be related. Should I ask him?

In the '60s the Clark campus had acquired a reputation as a haven for hippies in contrast to the orthodox environs of Holy Cross, the serious turf of Worcester Tech, or the respectable halls of Assumption College. But in fact, all four of these schools have invited me to Worcester. Rookie Quinn's father, it turns out, is a lieutenant on the force, and his son, who seems ready to shake apart with anger, must have grown up hearing mealtime stories about the pot smoking, rock scored antiwar demonstrations at Clark—the live-ins and love-ins. And here I was, I could almost read it on the young officer's face; here was the current transgressor-in-residence of public morality standing before him on the corner of Main and Allen streets at about 11:30 at night.

The four schools had gone together to form the Worcester Consortium for Higher Education. Their purpose was to pool funds and facilities and invite writers to their different campuses, each hosting a writer for a semester where he or she would work with students selected from the four institutions. In the fall semester, Galway Kinnell had held poetry seminars on the campus of Holy Cross.

"How do you like it here?" I had asked Galway. Earlier in autumn, I had driven over from my home in New York to attend a reading he gave on the Clark campus. Another part of the job was that consortium writers were to give public readings of their work at different locations around the city. But to say Galway gave a reading is not a fair description, for, as is his practice, he recited his luminous poetry with almost no reference to the printed page. Several years back, a mutual friend had introduced us, and now we were having a beer, after his presentation, in a bar near the campus.

Galway did not answer me directly. Having grown up in Paw-tucket, Rhode Island—part of greater Providence—the mill-town atmosphere of Worcester might have seemed familiar to him. The ramshackle nature of the place, its depression and falling-down, was a character similar to how I remembered Pawtucket from my own time in Providence at Brown University. The industrial exodus after World War II to the South had retreated through all of New England. We also share a friendship with Stanley Kunitz, and Galway mentioned that Worcester is the older poet's birth-place. He thinks Stanley hasn't been back to Worcester since he left for Harvard some fifty years before. I got the feeling that Galway didn't spend a whole lot of time here himself—maybe only showed up for his class at Holy Cross.

"What are you doing in Worcester?" Officer Germain might have asked Galway Kinnell.

"I am a visiting faculty member at Holy Cross," he would answer.

"Ah, Holy Cross, is it," Officer Quinn might have said. "Here, can we give you a lift to where you're staying? It's a cold night and the streets around here are full of suspicious characters who teach at Clark."

But where is Galway Kinnell while I am in this jail? Send for Norman Mailer! Get me out of this place! Today is my son's birthday, and here is his father, sending him good wishes from behind bars. I may seek the cloistered life, but I want some say in it, a choice of imprisonments.

"There's probably been a mistake," the booking sergeant said. He's a trim, dapper guy with an Italian name, and he's been casually observing the struggle the two cops are having with the steel cuff on my left wrist. My hand was growing numb. The sergeant's manner suggests a tolerance of all human folly and depravity. He's seen it all. Therefore, my innocence must strike him with the force of an April sun. At last he steps down from his desk and lends his own expertise. The steel bracelet falls open with a blessed relief.

"You're damned right there's been a mistake," I said. "A terrible mistake."

My arrest on the corner of Main and Allen streets was so obviously a mistake that the sergeant's regret has been made even more acute by the knowledge that he must continue the procedure; he has no other choice, his manner suggests. He is as much a victim of the process as I am. Sadly, he must lock me up until the district court meets in the morning where—not a smidgen of doubt on his face—justice will be done. But in the meantime, he'll just change the charge from "disturbing the peace" to "disorderly conduct." The silent, wide-eyed chorus of cops around him maintains such a fix on their Celtic moon-faces that I almost do the laughing for them.

Just like the movies, I'm allowed to make one phone call. A policeman pokes through the change I've just handed over for safekeeping and hands me the proper coin. The pay phone is mounted on the wall of a corner in the station house, above a broken-down sofa that has been shoved into the space beneath. In order to use the instrument normally, I have to lean on a seat cushion. "Get your knee off that couch," a voice commands. I stretch and dial the operator and place a collect call.

My wife is delighted that I have called her for a chat at this hour. She starts talking about our son's birthday, the plans for the party, which I will miss. I have to cut her off, and as I talk through her amazement, I am aware that I have become the focus of the station house's midnight improvisation. We are all in it together, the cops, my wife, and I, taking up our different parts and reading our lines. I am letter perfect; a careful rendition of the outraged citizen whose innocence has been impugned by the cruel destiny that hailed me at the corner of Allen and Main streets. I can feel the eyes of the chorus behind me lift to heaven. My wife gasps and something like respect edges her voice. Perhaps I have surprised her with recklessness, daring she had never suspected.

But I need help. The only person I know in Worcester is the chairman of the Clark English Department—the man who hired me. "Call him and tell him to get me out of this place," I tell her.

Jonas Gilman Clark founded his university in 1889, about ten years before another self-educated, self-made millionaire industrialist, Andrew Carnegie, set up his own alma mater in Pittsburgh. After success as a carriage-maker and a manufacturer of general hardware, Clark left his native Worcester in the 1850s to go west to California, where he made a fortune selling supplies to gold miners. Then came the Civil War with its entrepreneurial opportunities, and these profits were turned over and further compounded by his canny investments in government securities.

Meanwhile, Mr. Clark had also accumulated an enormous private library. He also acquired acreage along Main Street, about a mile and a half from where I am about to be locked up, on which he built a university in 1889, and where—some ten years later—the terms of his will established a near-separate institution given to the undergraduate study of the humanities rather than a graduate curriculum of the first school. If only Clark had given the place a more practical twist, as had Carnegie with his advanced trade institute, night classes for blue-collar workers, and home-making courses for their wives, I might not have been handcuffed and given a trip downtown to this Italianate dungeon.

"I am a visiting faculty member at the Clark Institute for Serious Mechanics and Useful Engineering," I could have said to Officer Quinn. A sudden warmth in his eyes would have thawed the icy bond between us.

In 1909 Sigmund Freud was lured from Vienna to Worcester with the promise of an honorary degree (plus 750 dollars) from Clark to address a mammoth congregation of world-famous psychologists, put together by the university's president, himself an eminent psychologist. William James showed up "just to see what Freud was like." Also on the panel were Freud's protégé and associate, Carl Jung, and during this meeting in Worcester, the two men deepened their suspicions of each other that were to widen into the schism that marks the practice today. About twenty years later, physicist George Goddard joined the Clark faculty and fired off the first liquid-fueled rockets into the atmosphere. So onto this launch pad of explorations into both inner and outer space, came this vagrant, unheralded fiction writer in the winter of 1978, looking for a space to make his own.

The Clark English Department had reserved a dormitory room for me—perhaps Kinnell had been offered similar accommodations at Holy Cross—but I wanted a space with a kitchen and a quiet corner where I could set up my typewriter. I had already begun looking for such a place several years before—a retreat from wife and children in which to do my work and pursue the illusive persona I wanted to be. The surroundings were not all that important; a cave, a tree house, or an island likes Crusoe's. How about a cell?

The small apartment on Benefit Street had one room, with a kitchen and bath, situated on the top floor of a dilapidated building a half-dozen blocks from the Clark campus. The previous tenant had left with the front-door lock, knobs and all, so my first order of business was to acquire and install a new set from a hardware store. The next was to get a bed, since the landlord-agent's interpretation of the term "furnished" did not include this appointment. I gave up my appeals and made up a pallet on the floor of my duffel bag stuffed with towels.

The chairman of the English Department, the same man my wife is waking up at midnight with the news that I am in jail, had greeted the descriptions of my apartment, especially my sleep-ing arrangement, with respectful awe. Clearly, my hardy pioneer spirit impressed him. Since Jonas Clark's day, the neighborhood around the Clark campus had badly deteriorated into a ghetto of the poor and the deprived, the miserable and the dangerous. But the atmosphere strangely appealed to me, and in fact I lived in a similar area in Providence while attending Brown. Curiously, the street name was the same—Benefit.

My traveling typing table fit neatly into a corner of the tiny kitchen, which was self-contained and snug like the cabin of a small sailing craft anchored in a protected harbor. The blizzard that raged outside shook the warped windows to sift small strands of snow upon the stained carpet. I was warm and dry and typing, and, in a way, Clark University was paying me to do this typing. The seminar students were alert and superior. My mornings and most of my afternoons were free. The resources of the university library turned up landmarks in my family's history, a geography that had been largely unmapped territory for me. I have been trying to revive my grandparents and my father so they might explain themselves to me, justify their movements across that old landscape where I had been abandoned. And, without intending to, I was seeking a reunion with my mother—at least on pa-per—piecing together an understanding of her careless love.

So, in these squalid rooms, I knew the transcendence all writers can experience. I was able to leave my hovel on Benefit Street and enter the abundant fragrance of my grandmother's kitchen in Kansas City, or I could climb onto my father's lap and drowse through a summer afternoon redolent with the odor of his sweat and the hazing of insects in tall weeds.

But outside it was a different atmosphere. The callous, uncaring attitudes of absentee landlords was evident on every street corner. The waste of their expedient greed encrusted every stair landing. Roaches and rats carried the messages of their indifference. Tenants were abused and cheated and their citizenry insulted by the presence of slow-moving police cars, armed and armored as if they had been manufactured for the civil wars of Central America but had somehow taken a wrong turn and wound up here in Worcester. In this neighborhood. Their continuous patrol of the streets became not so much an enforcement of its safety, but an enforcement of its residents—looking out for disorderly conduct. Or so I began to feel.

What I am saying is that when Officers Germain and Quinn stopped me on the way home from this party, a presumptuous anger has already proselytized my mind. I have put the discovery of my own abandonment, while incidentally abandoning my own family, together with the alienation I presumed on my neighbors' behalf, to make a false and self-serving alliance. After all, in the pocket next to my indignation, I carried the other half of a round-trip ticket that could take me out of these demeaning conditions. I was white and mobile. I could simply get into my car and drive two hours due west across the border to New York to the relief and refreshment of the old farm that my family and I have set up as our own private preserve. Not unusual, but I have been arrested for all the wrong reasons.

Meanwhile, my wife has awakened the English Department

chairman to tell him the writer he has hired as his contribution to the Worcester Consortium for Higher Education has just been thrown in jail for disorderly conduct. She is to tell me later that he was incredulous, but that he knew just the man to set it right, just the person to get me out of jail. This person was a faculty member who directed a program, funded by the U.S. Justice Department, which was supposed to raise the consciousness of the Worcester Police. In fact, this professor helped the chief of police get a master's degree. So, as the steel-barred door of my cell slides shut with the clang of a closure by Poe, buttons are being pushed for my release.

Perhaps Officers Germain and Quinn had suspected in my movement down Main Street a whole array of crimes that I had got away with up until then. Disorderly conducts. To claim that as a description of most writers' lives is a disingenuous plea at best. In the basement of Mr. Clemence's handsome building, I face the wall and multiple accusations.

I have deserted my children, not physically so much as spiritually and emotionally, committing the same desertion that I am trying to write about in *Last Stands: Notes from Memory*. Is this the same pattern that has begun to appear in the matter of abuse? Do the abandoned grow up to abandon? But the court will not permit irony. What are the extenuating circumstances? There are always extenuating circumstances. My purpose had been to make myself into a father worthy of their respect and love. In the meantime, their wounds have been deep.

More misconduct. I have lied to my wife. I have cheated on her. After more than twenty years of marriage, I have been disloyal to her in an affair with another woman. Could I plead the extenuating circumstances of a marriage gone stale? Of career and marriage going in opposite directions? An old story, a likely story—surely, the judge will turn a deaf ear. How would a jury of peers, picked at random from the neighborhoods around Benefit, find me? They would probably conclude that I had been picked up just in time.

"What time is it? Does anyone know what time it is?" my fellow prisoner down the cellblock has just cried out.

About four hours ago, I walked the half-dozen blocks from my apartment back toward the Clark campus and to the party that was given in my honor. A welcome to Worcester party. My tall farm boots crunched the snow of the narrow paths shoveled like a maze through the towering drifts. The frigid air pricked my nose with every breath. So the warmth and buzz of fellowship that spilled over the rooms of the large apartment warmed more than my bones. My host's girlfriend, it turns out to be her place, must have stuffed mushroom caps all afternoon. The platters were piled high. Plates of cheeses and meats, bottles of wine and whiskey; the buffet was more than ample. Moreover, local writers, most of whom had never heard of me, have been invited. My host's introductions vouched for me—he was a colleague at Clark. A couple of journalists were also present, including Ivan Sandorf, the former book editor of the *Worcester Telegram and Gazette*. He said he vaguely remembered one of my novels. So, passing from the subzero temperature outside into the glow of this candlelit reception, I pass through a kind of checkpoint. My papers have been found all in order—my identity has been verified. Headiness pumps through me though I have only had a single bourbon and water.

Maybe an hour later, I notice that both host and hostess have disappeared. Others also begin to wonder about their where-abouts. Neither has been seen at the buffet table, nor in the kitch-en preparing more treats. The bathroom is unoccupied. The party is coming apart, and people are running out of things to say to its unknown guest of honor. During an awkward calm in the conversation, we hear the sound of flesh striking flesh. The slaps are answered by cries that resemble the yowls of a cat whose tail has been stepped on. Pain or pleasure, we cannot tell which, but the sounds come from behind the closed door of a room across the central hallway of the apartment.

The party is glued in place by a fast-drying perplexity; a mixture of concern and amazement is fixed on every face. Then, one of the guests suggests we leave, that we give our hosts some privacy. She seems to know about their habits. Their unusual conduct has brought the party to an early end, and I am once again out in the cold. I bid good-bye to my newfound audience and start walking down Main Street toward the rendezvous with Officers Quinn and Germain at the corner of Allen Street.

The huge piles of snow pushed up by bulldozers resemble temples abandoned by a vanished race. The storm had been so enormous that army tanks had been brought in to clear the runways of Logan Airport in Boston. The pale, incognizant blink of streetlights cast a bluish patina over the deserted street that resembles an Arctic necropolis. But a block from my corner, a glow of life reflects upon the snow. The ground-floor windows of the Bancroft House of Health Care, a nursing home, are outrageously illuminated. Signs of life!

These windows are partially blocked by the snowdrifts. Their venetian blinds have been pulled up, and in the first window, as I pass by, I can see two people sitting on a couch. One is a registered nurse, wearing her cap, and both women are studying something at their feet. In the next window, as I have moved along, are a man and a woman who also look down at something below my line of vision from the sidewalk. What's going on? What has commanded this total concentration? My journal is in a side pocket of my parka, and I am prepared to be both witness and chronicler of any human event that comes my way. I walk up to the front door, beneath the porch light, and lean to the right to look through the second window.

Just as I suspected—it's an emergency! Someone's breathing is being restored. A man is bent over the body, doing mouth-to-mouth resuscitation. But it is all in vain, because it is a dummy being worked on and I am witnessing a class in CPR. My journal notes contrast the sober expressions of the humans with the merry whimsicality molded into the dummy's face. I note the unreal redness of the plastic figure's wig. All of this observation takes a few seconds. Then I turn around and continue on my way, walking in the street for the sidewalks are still blocked with snow.

At the next corner of Allen Street, the police cruiser pulls up beside me, nosing in toward a snow bank to effectively confine me. The two police get out. My lawyer is to speculate later that if the older, more experienced Germain had been in the passenger seat, he would have gotten to me first, and my arrest and imprisonment would probably not have taken place. But Germain was driving, so it was the younger, inexperienced Quinn, the son of a lieutenant on the force, who got to me. I was his.

Immediately, I knew why they had stopped me. They had been cruising south on Main Street and seen this suspicious character standing on the porch of the nursing home, wearing boots and a parka with the hood up, peering into one of the windows. If I had been at the wheel of the cruiser, I would have turned it around myself to come back and ask a few questions.

So, I told them what had been going on, what I had been observing. I suggested we all walk back and look in the window together to see what was taking place on the floor of the home's recreation room—to verify that I hadn't been spying on old ladies and gentlemen preparing for bed. They weren't interested, though they are to testify later that they did check out my story, but only after I have been hauled away to jail. I answered all their questions, handed over all of my identification. I was coming from a party, I told them.

"Have you been drinking, Professor?" Quinn asks sarcastically. His pale face seems to have thinned and he trembles, maybe from the cold. Germain has taken my driver's license and gets back into the cruiser. "What's going on?" I ask. "We do things differently here than in New York," he says. They have closed the doors and rolled up the windows. I am left in the well between the car and the snow bank, which towers above my head.

"Do you remember what the temperature was?" my lawyer will ask Officer Quinn at the trial.

"It was quite cold."

"And it was about eleven o'clock at night?"

"Yes, sir," Quinn answers.

"Where did you leave Mr. Masters when you and Officer Germain got back into your police car and closed the doors?"

"Beside the cruiser."

"Did you leave him standing between the snow bank and the cruiser?"

"Yes."

"Did you invite him, on this very cold night, while you were conducting your investigation, to sit in the cruiser with you?"

"No."

"Was the cruiser warm?"

"Yes, it was."

"Having been informed that he was Mr. Masters, that he was on the faculty at Clark, that he was on his way to his apartment, which was only a block away, that he had a valid license, you nevertheless left him to stand in that cold temperature between the snow bank and the cruiser while you got into the police car to do some further investigation?"

"That would sum it up quite well," Quinn responds.

"At that time you had placed him under arrest?"

"No."

"Up until that point, you hadn't felt that there were any grounds, at least, for charging him with disorderly conduct?"

"At that point, no, sir."

Then, several moments later, my lawyer is to ask, "By the way, Clark University has its own police department, doesn't it?"

"To my knowledge, it does."

"And it has a campus police?"

"Yes."

"With full powers of police on campus?"

"Yes."

"Did you use your radio to contact the campus police to come to the scene?"

"At no time did I contact the campus police," Quinn testified.

I was a suspect, and their manner scared me. Who I claimed to be was of no importance to these police. They had ignored the cards of membership that supported my claim to be a writer and a photographer. "What is it you do?" I could hear my brother-in-law's question on the night air. I seem to get arrested in Worcester for looking in the window of a nursing home. "Why don't you get a job?" my wife would ask. I'm trying to find a job but these cops have interrupted the search and left me standing outside in the cold on the corner of Allen and Main streets. In fact, they have taken my driver's license and gotten back into the cruiser. After a couple of minutes, I edged myself up on the fender of their car and pulled out a book from my parka. I had bought the book just that afternoon, and, using the glow of the street light over head, I began to read Susan Sontag's *On Photography*.

"Humankind lives unregenerately in Plato's cave . . ."
The doors of the police cruiser burst open.

"Why did you sit up on that police cruiser?" my lawyer is to ask
me during our first interview. He has a modest office on Harvard Street and his name is Richard Welsh. At this point in our
relationship, I know more about him than he does of me. In the
early morning hours after my eventual release into the custody
of a Clark faculty member, I had phoned a former classmate
who was practicing law in DC. In the 1960s Les Hyman had been
the chairman of the Massachusetts Democratic Party; so, he had
a book—almost—on everyone in the state, especially lawyers.
Obviously, this is a connection not available to my neighbors
on Benefit Street, but all the more reason that I use it—on their
behalf, I tell myself.

Les Hyman's book on Welsh notes that he is a Greek and Latin
scholar who taught these subjects in high school as he worked his
way through Boston College. Therefore, he is a Jesuit-trained and
full-fledged Roman Catholic, important credentials for Worcester.
He is the father of a large family. One child studies music. But
most important, my friend tells me on the phone, is that Welsh is
not from Worcester and has only recently established his practice
in the city—he's yet an outsider and has not been brought into
the cozy establishment that informs the local court system. But
he is savvy on the local bench. And one more thing, Hyman adds,
Welsh pumps iron on weekends.

"So, tell me," lawyer Welsh asks, "why did you sit on that
police car?" Welsh is a stocky man with thick shoulders and a
round Irish face. Even sitting, he seems to barely contain a lean
energy.

"I had this book, and I didn't know how long they were going to take." He is looking away, bored. "And it was cold," I

continue. Welsh looks back, getting interested. "Well, I guess I was just mad."

"Right!" He leans forward.

"And I was tired." His eyes are smiling. He waits eagerly for me to go on, to give him the right answer. "And there was no place I could sit down."

"Okay." One hand slaps the top of his desk. "Here's what I'm going to ask you on the stand, and here's what you're going to say. Mr. Masters, why did you sit on the fender of that police car? And you're going to say that it was your way of expressing a *mild* protest at the way you were being treated by the police."

"A mild protest."

"Right. The First Amendment of the Constitution covers such protest. The Massachusetts Supreme Court just reaffirmed this interpretation in a case. Remember, a *mild* protest." Then he shrugs and smiles good-naturedly. "Of course, this probably won't mean much in the district court but when we appeal that verdict to the superior court, the plea will carry some weight."

"It will? We're going to appeal?" The wheels of justice have already run over me, but not to worry. We're appealing.

"Of course," Welsh says. "The district court judges always listen to the cops' side. You'll get a guilty verdict, but then we'll appeal."

"We will?"

My advocate's eyes appraise me, evaluate my qualities as a client. Somehow the nature of this interview has been reversed. Finally, he says, "What does your freedom mean to you, Mr. Masters?" I've been seeking that answer for several years. In New York City. In Iowa. Now in the frozen streets of Worcester. Should I soil his clear-eyed, Jesuit view with my equivocations—my freedom at the expense of wife and children, the use of that freedom and the dubious value of the results? Welsh doesn't give up, and he gives the question an objective turn. "How much is an American citizen's freedom worth?"

"I was only in jail a few hours," I say.

"Ten minutes or ten years—it's all the same. It's all the same if you're unjustly imprisoned." He is lecturing me. He could probably say it in Latin, and I see him addressing the old Roman Senate, a little bulky in his toga, as he rises to defend this vagrant Celt, a peddler of romances. He's the right man, but first I have to get out of jail on the morning of February 17.

Which I am more than ready to do when the keeper shows up at my cell with his bunch of keys. It's a little after one o'clock in the morning, and I am no more satisfied to be holed up in this underground writers' retreat designed by George Clemence. I've admitted my crimes, pled guilty to desertion and adultery, arrogance and selfishness—hubris in the first degree. Now it was time I was released. I've been punished enough so slide back these bars.

The envoy from Clark University has arrived, and I am led upstairs to another part of the police station, the main lobby. Here, the faculty member who helped raise the consciousness of the Worcester Police greets me, and he turns out to be the genial host of the party I had left only a few hours before. He is very much at home in the station, calling officers by name, being greeted by others; hugs all around. My arrest has precipitated a jolly reunion. "Hello, Sarge," he says to one. "How's the wife?"

Meanwhile, the young woman whose unique martyrdom had caused the early break-up of the party, and which had put me on the fateful course toward Officers Quinn and Germain, waits on a bench on the far side of the room. She seems composed, her shapely legs crossed and one foot idly marking time, but as I approach, I note her pretty face looks swollen from crying. When

I sit down beside her, she takes a few ragged breaths and hiccups a sob or two, all of which I take to be a residue of the particular ecstasy that my arrest may have interrupted. "It's okay, Ruby," I say, patting her knee. "It's okay," I repeat, feeling that the injustice done me has stretched out to include her as well. The man who should be arrested stands free at the high desk across the way, trading jokes with a couple of policemen.

The sergeant sitting at this desk waggles a couple of fingers at me, and I approach. "Before court this morning," he says as he signs my release paper, "go to the probation office. It's just down the hall from the courtroom. Go see this guy." He writes the name on a separate slip of paper. "He can do something for you that will save you money." My host nods agreeably. He's worked out a deal for me—I have been given back my freedom because of his influence.

But I am not entirely convinced. On the ride back to Benefit Street, I watch and listen to my benefactor and his girlfriend from the backseat of his car. They chat cheerfully about my experience, how it was a terrible mistake and that it would all be over in a few hours. Everything would get back to normal, they both agree. But can I trust their definition of normality? On those classic scales that Justice holds, how far down must one side sink to raise the forgiveness or the approval of another. In human love, perhaps a similar formula is to be worked out, one that makes for a continual immolation of the heart. Montaigne would have speculated on these roles we play—the demeaning positions that we sometimes have to assume to enjoy an ephemeral freedom.

But it is nearly three o'clock in the morning, and I must not digress. When I get back in my apartment, I call Les Hyman, wake him in Washington DC, and ask him if he knows a good lawyer in Worcester.

Hyman has also instructed me to ask for a continuance, a postponement, when the court convenes at eight o'clock in order to engage a lawyer. But first, I look up the guy in the probation office recommended to me by the desk sergeant who had signed my release papers. The guy who can save me money.

This officer is peeling off the lid of a very large plastic cup of coffee, a burning cigarette stuck in one corner of his mouth. He looks like he's been up all night, too, and in fact, he already knows all about me. The folder with all the particulars of my arrest is on the countertop before him. He sips the coffee carefully, almost delicately, one pinky finger stuck out, as he opens up the thin dossier and reads. After a couple of swallows, he says, "There's nothing here. It's all a mistake."

"You're damned right," I say.

"Court convenes," he pauses to check his watch, "in half an hour. I have something for you that could save you money."

That phrase once more. Certainly, the system is admitting that Quinn and Germain were out of line. The system recognizes my innocence, and I'm being offered a deal that would save me money as it saves face for the system. How often, I wonder, has this alternative been used to settle such mistakes. How many mistakes have been made?

Meanwhile, he's been explaining the offer. In return for my tacit admission of guilt, made right now in the privacy of this office, I would be granted a "non-verdict" that would disappear from my record once I completed a probationary program of group therapy. He shrugs, as if to say that, in my case, this last requirement would probably be waived. I wouldn't even have to attend the sessions. His eyes fix me with a bleary collegiality—it's a simple, easy solution to the problem Quinn and Germain had put all of us in a few hours before. Just sign this paper, on this line. Simple.

The nightmare looks no different in the hurtful light of day, and I am exhausted. Yet, something makes me hesitate. An alarm works through the cotton stuffing in my head. Off the record or not, I will still be pleading guilty to a misdemeanor I have not committed. Most of my life may have turned on misdemeanors, my whole career a docket of disorderly conduct, but I had been a cold, cooperative, and solid citizen at the corner of Main and Allen streets. Moreover, Welsh is to tell me later that the deal offered me is a probationary program designed for juvenile first offenders—to give kids a second chance. Obviously, I fulfilled none of those requirements.

At this point in my journal, the entries spill over the pages with a righteous scrawl. My response before the weary probation office was no less idealistic. How could I face my students if I signed this? What of my honor? My integrity? What would I say to my children? It was my son's birthday. Is this the sort of gift I should give him—his father copping a plea? I did not offer my neighbors in the ghetto, but, I thought, if I accepted this offer, wouldn't it be to desert them once again? But the guy has already closed up my folder and turned away, taking an exhausted drag on his cigarette. He walks over to a file cabinet. He has done all he can to help me and to no avail. A sad case. It's going to cost me money.

Whatever majesty the law is supposed to have, the quality was absent that morning in the Worcester District Court. A comical version of Balzac by way of the Marx Brothers was in progress when I took my seat at the rear of the courtroom. I spotted Quinn, already there and in full uniform, truncheon and pistol holstered in the leather harness buckled around his waist. But for now, both accused and accuser become temporarily unified, a single audience for the acts being brought before the judge sitting at the front.

The accused seem to be unnecessarily trying out for roles for which they have already been cast. The vagrants and prostitutes, the petty thieves, and the others charged with conduct that had offended the City of Worcester and the Commonwealth of Massachusetts during the night might have been giving auditions, not so much to win roles but to garner evaluations of their performances in them. The district judge enjoyed every one, winking and nodding and smiling to convey his pleasure with the artistry of the pleas thought up by the different wretches who stood before him. "That's a good one," his affable shake of head suggested to the court clerk and the sergeant of arms who, in turn, relayed to the lawyers and the police and the rest of us the measure of this particular strolling player's routine. "Thirty days," the judge announced and cracked the gavel. The clerk rose to introduce the next act.

Quickly, in a matter of only two or three cases, we become aficionados, experts in the law and the tradition of this district court, this particular judge. Critiques were exchanged—one verdict compared to another. This performer had dropped a line or looked away at the wrong moment. Missed cues were unforgivable. "Six months!" The gavel smacked down. The guy got off easy, someone said—for Christ's sake, he'd waved his hands like he was selling vegetables. The gavel raised and lowered on the next case of bad behavior—a performance so poor that the judge had to hide his laughter behind his hand. The rest of us were embarrassed for the condemned. She should have worked harder on her lines. "Detained for psychiatric examination." Bang!

I had begun to enjoy the burlesque myself, laughing out loud at some of the egregious excuses offered for a moment's indiscretion, a fall from civic grace. Sometimes cops would double over, thump each other, in shared amusement. The court stenographer had to interrupt her record to wipe her glasses and her eyes. One actor said he hadn't known his wife had closed their bank account when he wrote and cashed that check at the MacDonald's he managed. Here's a good one, someone whispered. The man's story was eloquent, full of modern complexities—corporate insensitivity, a woman's revenge, how circumstance can suborn the best of motives. It was a tale grounded in contemporary angst and the place was riveted silent. The judge's face had grown long and his eyes turned heavenward. Then, *bang* went the gavel. "Six months in the workhouse, full restitution, plus damages." It had been a socko performance!

"*The Commonwealth of Massachusetts against Hilary Masters.*"

The call lifts me to the ceiling where I expect a yardarm to suddenly appear, and I am Billy Budd. All the crimes against family and myself pull me to my feet, and I want to shout out—to join all those condemned creatures who have preceded me—"Yes, guilty. I am guilty! Hang me. Better to be punished for the wrong crime than to go free of the others." But, of course, I ask for a continuance and it is granted.

"We're hiring our own recorder," Welsh tells me a month later. We're about to go to trial on the charge of disorderly conduct brought by Officer Quinn. "The tape they use in the district court sometimes gets erased." His look is of forced innocence. "This way our person will be sworn in and her record will be official. So we will have an exact transcript. For the appeal, you know."

In the meantime, advice has not been scarce. My wife had wished that I had taken the option, the plea-bargaining. Her brother had just been appointed to a minor political position in his hometown, and he hoped things could be kept quiet, for he suddenly had ambitions of his own. An older writer friend advised me, "Stay away from lawyers—read Dickens!" My lover in New York City patiently listened to my late-night phone calls and then assembled a complex of moral principles for my infantile indignation to climb. Not so much justice, but her continued favor waited at the summit.

We've had a change of judges too; not the merry hangman I had witnessed the morning after my arrest but an older judge because the court calendar had become overcrowded. "The verdict will be the same," Welsh assures me reasonably, "but it will be pronounced more pleasantly. This judge thinks of himself as a gentleman."

"But I will still be found guilty—pleasantly guilty."

He nods agreeably. "Then we will appeal to the superior court, which will have a jury. We will probably win that one. Then, we sue them?"

"We sue them? The cops?"

"You want to do that don't you? You're still mad, aren't you?"

"On what grounds?"

"False imprisonment. Malicious prosecution. Assault and battery." He holds up the color Polaroid I had had taken of my bruised wrist at a shop that did passport photos the day after my arrest. The flesh has since healed and shows no injury.

And everything else *has* gone back to normal, as I had been promised it would. My manuscript was almost finished. I had sent off a portion of it to Houghton-Mifflin for their new work contest, and they had asked to see more. I never mentioned my arrest to my writing seminar at Clark, but I think the students knew anyway; perhaps the colleague who had freed me had passed the word. Actually, both he and the department chair seemed a little perplexed, as my wife had been, that I had not taken the probationary deal. That I had hired a lawyer seemed to worry them also. How is it going, they would ask, a little distance in their voices. This visiting hack in residence was about to compromise the university's reputation. The Worcester Consortium for

Higher Education was going to be dragged through the papers. Why hadn't I just played along and accepted the deal?

In his testimony, Officer Quinn said that I had "climbed to the top of the snow bank and jumped onto the hood of the cruiser." The snow bank had been over my head.

"How did he land? asks Welsh.

"He landed on his behind," Quinn answers. I am watching the judge. His aristocratic features are solemn, not a flick of incredulity, not even a little amusement.

"He didn't jump with his feet on it?" Welsh persists.

"He didn't land on his feet, no."

Welsh asks Quinn to estimate my height and weight, and he makes a guess—about six feet tall and 170 pounds. Then, "Did he do any damage to it?"

"Not that I know of."

"Did you look?"

"I checked it. I could find no damage," Quinn answers.

Welsh has paused and looks for a long second in the direction of the bench. He is asking the judge how a man of my size and weight, could leap from a high snow bank and land ass-first upon a car hood without damaging it. Not even a dent, his glance insists. The judge looks down at his notes. Yes, yes, he nods impatiently. Let's get on with the hanging.

But, as it turns out, Officer Quinn and the commonwealth never had a chance. Both were represented that morning by an inexperienced law student working as an intern in the prosecutor's office. Perhaps the authorities were confident the system would take care of itself, that the procedure required no more experienced hand to steer it toward a guilty verdict. Or maybe they just didn't care, or, not all that familiar with Richard Welsh, they underestimated his Jesuitical yen for justice.

For another reason, I had already begun to feel a little sorry for Quinn earlier that morning. I had been waiting for Welsh in the small coffee shop of the courthouse before the court convened. The young officer appeared in the doorway, almost timidly looked around and then walked to a table in the center of the room where a group of policemen, Germain among them, sat talking and having coffee. Like Quinn, they were in uniform and waiting to give testimony on the charges of their arrests, but there the similarity ended. Quinn had pulled up a chair and sat down on the edge of the group. He leaned forward, alert to pick up the subject of their talk, to laugh as they laughed—to be part of the group. His eagerness to be a member of this company of seasoned officers seemed to vie with his insecurity in that company. A light clicked on in my head.

As the son of a lieutenant, he carried an extra integer on his badge number. This questionable credential, like an eleventh fingerprint, would always put the performance of his duty under a special review. The men sitting at that table, chatting easily among themselves might be skeptical of his very presence in their ranks because of this chance of biology. His awkward hankering to press himself into their fellowship, that caused his laughter to be just a little too loud, was familiar stuff to me.

My own father's fame and image has often been invoked by lazy or spiteful reviewers of my work. I have been judged and found guilty of an unsought nepotism—for even having the temerity to be published. The verdict, after more than a dozen books under cover, is still being handed down, and I wonder if the same was true of Quinn all those years before. He might be a lieutenant himself on the force today, but perhaps some of his colleagues yet sentence him to this peculiar confinement, this prejudicial judgment of his talent and ability.

When the manuscript I was trying to finish in Worcester finally found a publisher three years later (*Last Stands: Notes from Memory*, David R. Godine), Donald Hall wrote a wonderfully insightful review for the *New York Times Book Review* that commended the prose and the structure of this family biography, and he particularly singled out the way the figure of my mother emerged as the book's central character. Of the four characters in the book, both the mother and the grandfather surpassed the "father figure" in importance. He was only one of four characters. Yet, an editor on the book review, ignoring Hall's account of the book, falsely characterized the memoir. EDGAR LEE MASTERS WAS HIS FATHER the headline above the review proclaimed.

More recently, my second collection of short stories, *Success*, gave the anonymous reviewer on *Publishers Weekly* the chance for some cheap psychological analysis, spending most of the space to advance a theory of my supposed competitive relationship with the poet of *Spoon River* and how that relationship, obviously, influenced the title of the collection. As for the stories, they were barely mentioned.

Ivan Sandorf, the former book editor of the *Worcester Telegram*, has been called to the stand to testify on my behalf. Welsh questions him about my behavior at the party. Was I under the influence of alcohol when we all left at 10:30 the evening of February 16? No. How had I behaved? Like a gentleman. A key word in the courtroom that morning. Earlier, Welsh had asked me the question we had rehearsed in his office, "Mr. Masters, why did you sit up on the fender of that police cruiser?"

"Because I wanted to make . . ." some kind of protest, but what kind? On the stand, my mind had blanked out, and I couldn't think of the qualification Welsh had told me to say. The Supreme Court had said a citizen could make some kind of protest to his treatment by a policeman. It was covered by the First Amendment. But what kind was it? "I wanted to make a . . . *gentlemanly* protest to the way I was being treated."

Not the right word, but Sandorf told me later it had been very effective. Looking on from the courtroom, as he waited to testify, he said the judge's head had raised slightly and, with a smile, he had scribbled on his notepad. "Right then," Sandorf told me, "I knew you were home free."

And so it went. Welsh's acute questioning, Quinn's inconsistencies, and the student prosecutor's inexperience clearly frustrated the judge's desire to find me guilty. "Where in your case," he finally asked the other lawyer, "where is there the substance that I can use to find for the Commonwealth?"

"Well, your honor," the young lawyer answered. "If the police cruiser had been called to a scene of an emergency when the defendant was sitting on it, he would have constituted a hazard to public safety." The judge had begun shaking his head halfway through. "No, no," he said, and with a light tap of the gavel, he found me not guilty.

But I was guilty as charged. My conduct had been more than disorderly. I had been fleeing the scene of many crimes when temporarily stopped at the intersection of Main and Allen streets on the night of February 16. My rush toward that freedom, and the validation I hoped to find within it, had collided with a similar urgency of Officer Quinn's. He proved his worth squeezing an extra notch on the handcuff around my left wrist, giving me the chance to thumb my nose at all those who had questioned my identity, who had not accepted my credentials. Revenge is a cold supper.

The morning has become clear in Worcester and the air fragrant with the Earth's warming turn toward spring. Richard Welsh and I stand on the steps of the courthouse. The city of Worcester seems to be laid out before me. "Now it's our turn," he says and his eyes are merry.

In the Cards

All that summer and into the fall, the Pauleys would leave their house and walk to Independence Avenue, where they would cross that busy thoroughfare to follow the bend of Benton Boulevard around past the Chief Theatre and to the top of our block in Kansas City. Usually it would be after seven o'clock, supper done and dishes washed and put up in most houses, and my grandmother would have cleared the dining room table and given the dark mahogany veneer a quick wipe as my grandfather lined up two pencils, freshly sharpened, next to the notepad. Then he would open the deck of cards and do the first of several shuffles before smacking the neat mass down on the tabletop with an "ahem" as he cleared his throat. He was ready for battle and could have cocked a gun.

How they met Fred and Jenny Pauley and how they began meeting weekly to play bridge remains a mystery to me; my interests at twelve were model airplanes and a girl named Mary Lou in the seventh grade at Scarritt School. So I wasn't paying attention to these weekly games beyond my appointed duty of serving the homemade wine my grandfather kept in an old bourbon barrel in the basement. The Pauley's house four blocks away and across Independence Avenue was at a distance beyond casual encounter, out of the neighborhood, so I'm guessing my grandmother may have first made contact through her political affiliation with the Pendergast organization of the Democratic Party. Or maybe it was a woman's group such as the Daughters of Isabella, of which she served as president. What Fred Pauley did for a living I cannot recall; he may have been retired, though that status would not have been likely then. Every morning my grandfather would walk downtown to the city hall where he would take up his pen as an accountant in the water department, inscribing ledgers with his immaculate script. Family talk was that my grandmother had secured the job to get him out of the house.

"Here they come," I would alert my grandparents from the front porch. The Pauleys had turned at the top of our block and begun walking down the sharp incline of Roberts Street. Almost hand in hand, I want to say, but certainly in step with each other. Both roundish figures, healthy looking. Fred Pauley wore rimless glasses, and his appreciable paunch seemed to steer his progress confidently. Jenny Pauley was also on the plump side with a prettily featured face. She was a woman of many handkerchiefs, always had one tucked into the sleeve of her blouse, pinned on her left shoulder, or readily available in her purse to shake out freshly and dab at the perspiration on her brow or in the crease of her nose. She raised a fragrant dusting about herself.

My grandfather read both the *Star* and the *Post* thoroughly on the front porch in good weather and in the large wingback chair by the dining room pocket door in winter. He read every square inch of both papers. Reading had been the means of his self-education and his self-taught mastery of civil engineering, so I suspect he learned the rules of contract bridge from the syndicated columns published in one of the newspapers by Eli Culbertson. In the same way, he had learned how to make wine from the *Encyclopedia Britannica* shelved near the radio in the living room.

One fall he had all of us, including my mother home for a visit, pressing grapes in the basement, sieving their juice into the large barrel he had bought from a distillery put out of business by Prohibition. My job was to serve this wine during certain intervals of play, along with the pound cake my grandmother would have made that afternoon. Sometimes Jenny brought something from her oven. The riffle and slap dash of the cards would be suspended, and my grandfather would review the score he kept on the pad at his right hand. Almost always, my grandparents would be ahead, mostly due to his play, for he played the game to win—the only one at the table so committed to defeating an opponent. It was a contest he pursued as vigorously as he had when going after the Sioux or the Nez Perce on the frontier. For the others it was a social occasion, especially for my grandmother, who was starved, I think now, for some easy exchange with people not related to her political interests. Nor can I recall my grandparents making casual conversation between themselves on their own; their words to each other were always honed on the practical concerns of home maintenance, taxes, and voter registration. Fred Pauley never said much but became an amiable, good-natured chorus to the cardplay and talk, his firmly hitched belly just rising over the horizon of the dining-room tabletop.

My grandfather continually corrected Jenny or my grandmother on some lapse in their play, reminding them that each trick taken or lost had its particular consequence. He shared with them the tips he had learned from Culbertson's newspaper column that week. For me, his authority in these instructions was validated by the heavy gold watch that hung in his vest pocket, a timepiece he had won in a poker game on the Panama thirty years before. That earlier game, and all its inherent dangers, had been the subject of one of his colorful stories told to me at bedtime. The glare of his cool blue eyes during one of these lectures to the women would still the room, even seemed to silence the wheeze of the cicadas in the elm trees on the street outside.

"Let's see what you have, now," he would say after he had won a bid and as he aligned the cards of the dummy my grandmother had put down. A rasp of skepticism filed his voice, and it was the sound of someone accustomed to disappointment by life's disclosures. He carefully ordered my grandmother's so-so display of the different suits. Actually, she had a good sense of the game and was an effective partner without seeming to pay much attention to the play, and it was this offhand negligence while signaling her hand or taking a trick that would gall him, affront his mastery of a Culbertson rule.

"I clearly signaled the Blackwood convention with the four no trump bid," he said one evening with barely contained ire. He had just lost an attempt at a grand slam bid, and Fred Pauley pulled the spent cards together to shuffle them for the next deal. "What's that make the score, Tom?" he asked. His glasses glinted in the light from the ceiling fixture.

"Yes, yes," my grandfather replied as he carefully penciled in the new figures. "You're pulling even."

As I served more wine, my grandfather only drinking water (the wine-making in the basement was his challenge to Prohibition, what he considered the government's infringement of freedom), Jenny Pauley asked for more information on the new people across the way—what was the latest gossip?

"I guess you can add Mr. Stevens up the street to the list," my grandmother drawled with a little laugh. "That scooter he's always working on was parked in front of their house all afternoon Tuesday."

"He used a gas engine from an old washing machine," my grandfather told Fred Pauley. Admiration commanded his voice. "Got the design from a piece in *Mechanics Illustrated*." The table went silent, as if everyone was trying to find a place for this information in their daily concerns.

Mr. Stevens's contraption had become a feature of that summer, and the scooter's cacophony burst in the sultry air of Sunday afternoons like the sounds left over from some dreadful conflict. The blat of its unmuffled engine started and then stalled, started and stalled. It was a large, unwieldy assembly sheathed in thick plywood and painted green. Letting the scooter coast downhill would start its engine so it roared into life, full speed, and then abruptly stopped when he pulled it in at a curb to make adjustments. Once or twice he rode it all the way to the bottom of the block to make a U-turn in front of Joe Orto's grocery and then rush up the street like a Roman legion coming home, Mr. Stevens holding on for dear life, and his face the color of ashes. Then suddenly, the engine quit and he pushed it into the curb to continue his endless tinkering. By summer's end he had lost the attention of my playmates and me; all the kids in the block, and even his own children, wandered off to fly kites in the park three blocks over. He was left alone with his toolbox open and various tools and gauges arrayed on the sidewalk as he bent over the machine in the evenings, still plenty of light. One day, the scooter had stalled in front of the house across the street.

The Watsons had moved in from Oklahoma in the late spring. Mr. Watson sold Kelly tires to filling stations on a route that took him as far as Joplin and Booneville, and, as my grandmother reported to Jenny Pauley, local tradesmen began to appear, pull their vans in at the curb, and take a very long time to make their deliveries inside. The trucks of plumbers and electricians, a local carpenter, and even the little Ford from the flower shop next to the Chief Theatre waited silently, their motors off as the job was done inside. What Mrs. Watson looked like, Jenny asked more than once, was never very clear for she rarely appeared outside the house. "Well put up," was my grandmother's description.

"Let's play cards," my grandfather interrupted the talk and cut the deck for Fred Pauley to deal. Bids were made, tricks taken, and suits made or failed. My grandfather meticulously added up the scores. The days grew short, and I could no longer spot the Pauleys as they turned down the top of our block, but the scrape of their feet in the twilight on the cement steps as they mounted our terrace would announce their arrival. My grandfather had begun to keep his suit jacket on in the evenings and had turned on the furnace to initiate the seasonal contest waged with my grandmother over the thermostat setting. His bouts with malaria and yellow fever in the tropics made him push the temperature high.

One evening my grandmother met the Pauleys at the top of the steps to our porch with a finger across her lips. She nodded toward the house across the way. "That's Mrs. Stevens from up the street," she said softy to answer their silent questioning. A woman sat on the top step of the Watson's first terrace, and she had just leaned forward to light what looked like one of those small candles that illuminate an altar. Then she uncapped a shiny thermos and poured something from it into a cup, coffee or maybe soup. Another woman appeared and my grandmother identified her as the wife of the florist. Yes, Jenny Pauley agreed, that was her all right. She knew her too. She must have walked around from Benton Boulevard.

This second woman sat down on the steps and unwrapped a glass bowl and began to spoon its contents into her mouth. Jell-O. She also had brought a candle with her and lit it, and the two women began to chat easily in the candlelight.

A truck with "Northeast Plumbing" lettered on its door coasted into the curb just below the house, stopped, and the engine and lights were turned off. A woman got out and walked up the street to join the first two, who waved in greeting. They all seemed in good spirits; it was like some sort of women's club meeting on the Watsons' front steps. The newcomer laughed at something one of them said. She had also brought a candle and lit it and then passed around what looked like cookies. The flames of the candles flickered merrily in the deepening shadows, and the faces of the women would be suspended briefly in their illumination, leaning forward and then back, in and out of the darkness. Talking quietly.

"Why, it's like sentries setting up," Fred Pauley said.

"You could say that," my grandmother replied and hummed a little something.

"Maybe she'll come out," Jenny Pauley said. "We'll see what she looks like."

"Well, are we playing cards or not?" My grandfather had come to the front door and spoke through the screen. The Pauleys and my grandmother almost meekly obeyed his summons, filing indoors and taking their places. He had carefully readied the dining room table for the evening's contest. They cut for dealer and the cards skimmed across the table. As I served the wine during a pause in the play, I checked the scene across the street. The candles illuminated the women as they talked among themselves; a fourth one burned on the bottom step. The next time I looked out they were all gone, but the candles continued to guard the night. Toward the end of the month, a large moving van pulled up across the street, the Watsons' furniture and belongings were loaded up, and they disappeared.

"There!" my grandfather exclaimed as he trumped a trick. "There!"

Several months later on a balmy December afternoon, I tested a newly completed model plane from the top of our terrace. It was a jaunty bi-wing SE-5, the British fighter from the World War, and I had wound the rubber motor tight and set it aloft. It rose in the air, lifting my heart on its tissue-paper wings as its propeller spun into a luminous disc. The little plane flew serenely and astonishingly over the head of Fred Pauley, who had just come down the sidewalk and seemed to have materialized in the broad daylight. He was alone. The two of us followed the plane's flight across the street and, when the propeller stopped, watched it glide into the thick weeds of the vacant lot next to the house that had been the Watsons'. Two women schoolteachers lived there now.

As if the plane's soft landing had satisfied something inside of him, Mr. Pauley turned back to me, his glasses two round mirrors. "Your people about?" he asked. I don't remember where my grandparents were; it was a Sunday and my grandmother was most likely at some political meeting. Now that I think of it, my grandfather was in the backyard, cutting and burning brush, one of his weekend chores.

"It's just come over the radio," Fred Pauley was saying, "and I walked over in case you weren't listening. The Japanese have bombed a place called Pearl Harbor. It's in the Hi-waiian Islands."

Later that evening my grandfather said, "Here it is." We were hunched over a volume of the encyclopedia next to the radio as an announcer told about the attack. "The islands of Hawaii, formerly known as the Sandwich Islands," my grandfather read, "named so by James Cook in honor of his friend Lord Sandwich—they're composed of nineteen islands and atolls and extend some fifteen hundred miles in the northern Pacific." He thumbed down the page, whispering to himself. I heard my grandmother move a pot on the stove and open and close the door on the new refrigerator from Montgomery Ward.

"What about Pearl Harbor?" I asked him finally.

"Killed and eaten, by God," he said. "James Cook. The natives on Hawaii ate him." His laughter was dry.

"When was that?"

"In 1779." He continued to stare at the page, and a wary look slipped into his expression as if the information on the page had become unbelievable.

"What about the Japanese?" I asked. He had shaved for dinner and I could smell the witch hazel he usually doused on his face. He wet the tip of a finger and turned a page.

"This is it," he told me, finding a paragraph. "On the island of Oahu the navy set up a dry dock in a bay called Pearl Harbor. They repair ships there." I thought of Mr. Stevens making adjustments on his scooter; it still wasn't running right. "The navy took the place over from the Hawaiians in 1908."

"1908," I repeated as if to make the date more contemporary. So it was an old place, Pearl Harbor. Why would anyone want to bomb it? Just then my grandmother called us to dinner. She had made a salmon loaf with white sauce and parsnips sautéed in butter. The bridge games petered out in the winter, and the Pauleys no longer showed up, no longer walked down Roberts Street together, as if something had happened to keep them on the other side of Independence Avenue.

Years later, from the window of a pensione in Sienna, I looked out on candles burning in the necropolis of a cemetery on a distant hill, and I thought of Mrs. Watson standing in the darkness inside her house and looking out at the glitter on her terrace, waiting for the candles to burn out, waiting for the scold of that vigil to pass.

A Day in
Burgundy

This morning I left St. Symphorien-de-Lay to meet the Loire just south of Roanne, and I will follow this beautiful river up to Digoin, a distance of about sixty kilometers on Route D982. It has been a lovely day in Burgundy: June weather in France, the dense aroma of ripening fields as their green and yellow carpets of trefoil and wheat unfold in the sunlight to be caressed by the shadows of close-flying cumulus clouds.

In the distance are low-slung farmhouses in the manner of old Roman villas, some with red-tiled roofs—some might very well be old Roman villas. Then, my little Ford is abruptly enclosed by a village. Buildings and high walls make a narrow corridor of the route, their clay surfaces reinforced by pebbles called *pierres dorees* because of their yellowish luster. At one corner, the knife-sharp edge of a town house projects like the prow of a stone ship, as if becalmed centuries back. It could cut me in two if a strong enough wind came up, so I carefully steer around it and come into the neat, open space of the village's square with its ubiquitous tablet dedicated to "les enfants de la patrie." A farmer in a blue jacket and cap and wearing high, black work boots, marches resolutely across the space toward the village's three or four stores, a *poste* and a *tabac*, lined up on the far side of the square. He is a countryman, French and probably a realist, so he does not recognize the catastrophe that might have happened to me at the corner behind him. Then, just as suddenly, I am back in the open countryside.

Since leaving Italy, many of these small French towns have tempted me to linger in them and snoop about their byways. Each one, according to my guidebook, offers an item for the serious tourist: a church with an interesting Ascension on its tympanum, something remarkable on another's lintel, or a pleasing view of a chateau (not open to the public) where a twelfth-century abbot of Cluny was born. But I am traveling not sightseeing; I stop only for meals and sleep. Yet, I am in no hurry. The wand of the speedometer rarely rises to the red line, and I have no particular schedule but loaf a little closer each day toward Luxembourg from whence my return flight to America departs. The curiosities, the historic sites en route cannot tempt me—I am my own tourist.

Strange to go for days without conversation. Can one get out of practice talking, forgetting how to shape the sounds and assemble them into meaningful sentences—into something more than mere communication? Of course I have ordered meals and asked for a room at night, but these exchanges exercised only a utilitarian grammar, a Berlitz fluency that evaporated like the morning dew on the hood of my car. With little ceremony, a concierge or a waiter tactfully restored my isolation to me, and though a storekeeper's eyes might suddenly glisten with interest, it is also clear to her that I am a traveler off the track and nearly out of season. She holds back her curiosity.

So I make this journey within the three containers of my small car, my lack of language, and my mind. But these restrictions also grant me a curious freedom of speculation and an open range of thought; a liberty of movement within memory and imagination that has no limits though I may never get anywhere. This habit of mine to seek solitude within a community has left many behind; lovers and children, all paradoxically exiled on their own home turf. I have viewed them from afar, from the road that turns within me, and though some sites are very attractive, I do not often tarry.

My time in Italy might have caused the curious pilgrimage I am now making in France. From my base camp in Radda in Chianti, I made forays into Volterra, Sienna, Florence and places in between. Images were collected; my journal grew fat with observations. Some of its pages even press wildflowers picked in the fields. I worked hard to speak the language within the high walls of medieval hill towns. I became clotted with pasta and Michelangelo. I gorged on the postures of chic *florentina* who, in the burst of a Vespa, become deliciously practical as they hopped on the seats behind their boyfriends. The ceramic miens of Etruscan couples soothed me as they lounged on their tomb lids, waiting for passage to that All-Night Banquet. So, I have a satchel full of menus, and I have made the rounds. I have explored the vestibules and wings of the museum that is Tuscany.

The evening before I leave Italy, I open this letter in the garden of the *fattoria* where I stay and read my daughter's angry words in the amber twilight. The dramatic light on the hills beyond and around this vineyard limns the same flatness of background that Martini and Giovanni di Paolo painted with such exquisite exactness in the fourteenth century. Their ignorance or even contempt for perspective made them realists—this is the way the landscape actually looks! My daughter's words tear at my heart, and, for relief, I have looked away to locate myself in this landscape, for its appearance has never changed. Her attack questions our whole history and my affection for her. I am mystified and hurt, especially because, lately, I have been her only advocate within the family. Something I have written her has caused this outburst—my words, in the arc of their posting, have fallen short of their meaning, my intention. A misconstruction has occurred; yet, her unstoppered fury is so intense as to suggest a long-endured ferment, an old wounding that has never healed. Our relationship has not been what it has seemed.

My last evening in Radda, in Italy, I dine at a local *tratorria* called Miranda's. It is a picturesque place and has become a regular stopover for package tours. When I arrive, several huge busses are already parked before the restaurant, their engines patiently digesting their essence, as their passengers dig into the *tipico cucina* inside. They are English and German diners, or so the origin tags on the rear end of the busses indicate.

The place is entered through the kitchen, where women of several generations prepare vegetables, wash dishes, and attend pots on the large black stove. Miranda, an overblown version of the actress Colleen Dewhurst, conducts me to a small corner table and takes my order. Carefully, I recite my rehearsed Italian, for I wish to set myself apart from the other patrons who stick to their own languages. They ask for "green salad" or "Käse"—some merely point at the menu items. The English seem amused by their own arrogance, but I think I detect a kind of surliness in the Germans' tone. You Italians, they seem to imply, must remember a little German from the last time we were through here in 1944. But the language we speak doesn't seem to matter to the help.

From my table, I can look directly into one corner of the kitchen where two women wash dishes at a large slate sink. A third woman fills plastic bottles with water from the tap. These bottles all bear the labels of popular mineral waters: Fuggi, Panna—and for those diners who prefer the sparkling spring water of the French Alps—Evian. Similarly, a fourth woman decants wine from a raffia-wrapped jug into funnels inserted into bottles with labels that correspond to the *listi dei vini*. Whether Barolo Mascarello or Chianti Ruffino, it's all the same wine but priced appropriately to each bottle's label.

An English couple circumspectly objects to their Barbaresco San Lorenzo arriving at table already uncorked. But the waitress, a demure child whose features might have been sketched in by Donatello, pours the stuff and waits patiently for them to order their meal. It is a lesson that Italy teaches the naïve and unwary; we all get the same fare, no matter how fluently we might order something else.

But it is an old lesson, and I am weary of its teaching. By *dolchi*, I am more than ready to leave Italy and this table. The rigid routine of antipasto, primo, and secondo has become oppressive. Standardized. The historic guile has made me impatient, and the uniformity of façades has blanked out my interest. The square marble fronts slapped onto rude brick churches are like the ornate faces of old western emporiums nailed together to promote the hardware or the ecstasy to be found inside.

So for several days I have been drifting through France, aimlessly choosing each fork in the road, making random selections from menus, once sharing the plat du jour at a truck drivers' *relais*. I don't have to work hard at the language here in France; on the contrary, I seem to have become speechless, embraced a self-perpetuating silence as I noodle along toward Digoin. My child's letter lies in my pocket, and I am trying to sort out the circumstances of this painful rupture, this misunderstanding. To order ideas and then to express them requires a mind disciplined to discern differences. No labels are needed. Human thought implicates a self, but this self often becomes self-important and gets in the way of clear thinking, genuine feeling. It wants to be noticed. Perhaps I have committed this folly? My sense of my self as "the father" may have only addressed her, put the imprint of this persona on the exchange rather than speaking directly to her in a simple fluency learned by the heart. I may have made myself extrinsic to her concerns.

Lately, I have been thinking of the computer as an extrapolation of this self, or as close as mathematics can get to it—this externalization of the human mind. On the road to Digoin, I have opened this file, if you will, in order to avoid my daughter's letter in the same way I had looked away toward the Tuscan hillsides. Shouldn't we be a little wary of this linguistic instrument taking over the mind's meanderings, the self's playful associations of ideas and impressions? Soul's work. This electronic, booted-up tool of materialism would much impress Locke and his gang, but isn't it one more device to separate mind from self, from soul? And what a beguiling trick we may have played upon ourselves, for, with the flick of a switch, we have become the passive audience of our own conceits, as we install a governor on the half-awake, half-dream mind that has been freewheeling, if not free-willing me, down Route D982.

The Loire joins the Arroux at Digoin, and I am offered a choice of four roads to take: one due east to Macon, two to the left that accompany the Loire's westerly bend, and a northern route that strikes out along the banks of the Arroux. My Ford homes in on this one, Route D994, with Autun about seventy kilometers ahead. A likely spot for a picnic lunch. Fields of grain still play out on either side of the road, but here and there the staves of vineyards begin to offer more static chords. A purplish blur has appeared in the left corner of my windshield. Le Morvan, my map indicates. This geological wonder rises nearly three thousand feet and covers thirteen hundred square miles of forests, rocky gorges, and fast-running streams. The road, like all French roads, is clearly marked and well maintained. The air is fresh. The Ford hums. My destination is plainly before me.

Not all my excursions in Italy were made to the usual tourist sites. I also poked into the dusty corners inside my head, a store-house of useless artifacts and unverified illusions, and these tours were often guided by William Barrett's *Death of the Soul*, a book I had packed in my duffel. His witty discourse with Kant, and particularly his references to the computer, has encouraged my own awkward grabs at the ultimate question. The final disgrace. How can the infinite mind transcend, go beyond, what might be called its finite predicament? The original "how come" question. The cruel paradox given us by the same folks who brought us the big bang and to whom the ingenious orthodoxy of the computer seems to offer a solution. To keep memory accessible forever might be the long-sought answer.

Barrett describes a spider spinning its web outside a window of his study. He wonders what kind of mind the spider has, the nature of its consciousness. "We humans are farther along the scale of evolution, perhaps, but in our own way we are as finite and our mind as attached to its own conditions as the spider's to its own. We spin the brilliant web of our scientific concepts, but we cannot step beyond it." We *impose* (a favorite Kantian usage) our imaginations, our soul's yearnings, upon the material, finite world to create models of paradise such as St. Mark's, to construct the imperishable luminosity of poetry, or to seek the split-second divinity of orgasm. But now, with the computer, we can put up the reflection of our genius on screens, store them in eternal memory banks to achieve a kind of secular deliverance and resurrection of that genius. That's the idea.

The direction taken by the soul's eternal life is all important. The Greeks and Romans and others seem to go underground, but Christianity has always gone up, true believers winging af-ter Jesus—the first Big Bird—on His flight heavenward. And so on. Some of this metaphor's success must be due to the envy all earthbound creatures have of birds' flight, but only humans were given the understanding, with its concomitant pathos, as to why we cannot get off the ground. We are heavier than our imaginations, and the revolutions of the globe keep us pinned within the smothering embrace of Mother Earth. Without this reasoning of the problem, Icarus would have remained an unknown malcontent and the Wright brothers would have stuck to bicycles. There'd be no interesting Ascensions to check out over tympana.

But now we are going in a different direction—out. Outside and into the ethos. The mind radiates into a kind of all-embracing mimesis that, if it does not offer salvation, seems to guarantee a place of eternal salvage. Computer networks are becoming elysian dumps where the faithful can be uploaded forever and ever. Amen, if not hallelujah. But, like Barrett's spider, have we only just spun another fine web that, with all its fabulous constructions and glowing synapses, still limits us, keeps us earthbound, passive worshippers as we hack away at our own reflections? The mind may be put on file forever on the Internet, but the soul is left behind because it cannot be described—not even Plato, nor anyone since, could program it—so this inner self, with all its pitiful awareness of its container's vulnerability, is left behind. All the old-time religions, at the very least, promised we could take the soul along—no matter in what direction we were destined to go—but there's no room for it on the hard drive.

As I near Autun, the blur seen through my windshield has enlarged, the blues have purpled deeply with patches of bright greens and granite gray, and the scale of the Morvan Massif becomes even more dramatic as the flat terrain of the Arroux basin runs ahead to abruptly meet its wall. The three-thousand-foot Haut-Folin rises like a huge dam on my left, and for the second time this morning, I feel a little threatened; but the great sea that lay behind this huge extrusion has drained into the Seine basin long ago, and I safely enter Autun. If I had looked away, had not seen it, would this enormous upheaval of granite really exist? Or say, once observed, did my eyes give the topography its marvelous colors? Is this mass only an arrangement of grays? No such philosophical whimsies can qualify the existence of my daughter's letter. It lies in my jacket pocket to be read again and again, to replicate its anguish and anger, its colors indelible.

Autun is noted for its Romanesque treasures, but I ignore them according to my new habit and set up my picnic in the Roman theatre near the old town walls. I put down the items of my lunch on the worn stone seats of what might have been the "family circle," if the Romans had such a ticket. The roasted half of a chicken I picked up in Digoin is still warm and fragrant with tarragon and lemon. The small round of chèvre and the pear compose a pleasing sonata of forms in the open air. When I break into the crusty demi-baguette, I hear again the cheerful greeting of the proprietor in Gueugnon, a half hour ago, when I opened the door of her *boulangerie*. "Bon Jour, m'sieur!" The half-drunk Rhone, left over and corked from yesterday's picnic near Valence, has come into its own while rolling about the back seat of the car.

I imagine the Romans, fifteen thousand of them according to the Michelin guide, leaning forward in these seats to catch the bawdy fun of a road company doing Plautus. But then at play's end, they would emerge from this theatre into Gaul—not Rome. For a couple of hours, they could believe they were in the center of the empire, of their universe; yet, how sad they must have become, how keen their feeling of exile, as they came to their senses on the walk home. To refer to W. C. Fields—an authority that Plautus would certainly have respected—it would have been similar to coming out of Olivier's *Hamlet* to find you were still in Philadelphia. Augustus founded this city (he gave it his name, Augustodunum), and his intent was to build a sister city to Rome, a reproduction of his imperial capital. This theatre, for example, was the largest one in all of Gaul.

So no matter its grandeur, this colonial outpost was still an outpost, only a copy, an imitation of the original and, in fact, one put down in hostile territory. The Roman impulse to press its own image on a conquered land is not all that different from an adult imposing his character on a child's mind or the mind booting up its self-definition on an electronic tabula rasa, which, if it is the ultimate tool of materialism, surely must be the ultimate vanity mirror. The motivation of all colonialism is to duplicate and therefore perpetuate the parent consciousness, filtered through the ego. Plautus wrote of this obsession—so did Milton, Dickens, O'Neill. It's a long list.

Some years ago, my wife, another child, and I drove from New York to Santa Fe, New Mexico. Several days out, we stopped off to visit friends who had moved to a small town in southern Illinois. All day we had driven through fields of soy beans and corn punctuated by the bobbing heads of oil rigs, bringing up the concoction of other, more ancient vegetation. Near evening we pulled into this dilapidated village by the tracks of the Wabash Railroad. The hamlet's several stores leaned into each other, and a two-pump gas station glared starkly out from beneath a bay illuminated by bare bulbs. Across the street, an empty bank dared the ghosts of the Barrow Gang. A battlement of enormous grain silos rose from across the railroad tracks. From miles away, these gigantic constructions give the unknowing traveler the impression that a prairie metropolis lies just ahead, a place with all the amenities of civilization, but close up, these concrete, eyeless volumes often reign over near-deserted junctions of road and rail like the temples of a vanished race—of a people that had outgrown their ability to sustain themselves.

Our friends live in a large, rambling house built across the tracks from the granary by the man who had owned the local lumber mill—both now out of business. They keep a peculiar squalor, a kind of disinterested dishevelment that indicates an indifference to the usual routines of daily life and housekeeping. He is a sculptor but works as a draftsman in a nearby plant that designs and manufactures electronic devices for missiles. But this is only a job, for it is clear his real work takes place in a second-floor bedroom overlooking their backyard, the railroad tracks, and the silos.

He is a mathematician-sculptor, and in this back room he is piecing together the model of a conception that is intended to rise from these plains and equal—no, exceed—the size of the silos outside the window. "It is to be an art form that is not to be viewed objectively," he tells us. "Nor from without time, but which the viewer steps into and views from within. Consequently, the art changes with the viewer and time of its perception." He wants to enclose the whole town. Maybe more, his look suggests.

This construction takes up the entire room, the whole cubic volume of its space, and to view it "properly," we must fit ourselves within it. The sculpture is made of metal pipe, plastic sheets, pieces of mirror, and colored vinyl scraps and patches like a playground's maze, and our daughter responds appropriately, her spirits rise. It has been a long day for her in the cramped seat of the car. But no artistic whimsy has produced this work. Every fuse of plastic to metal, every joint of aluminum tubing, each placement of clear and colored segments, every positioning of mirror has been posited and proved by a mathematical formula. Pages of algebraic computations lie scattered about the floor like the wrappings of an enormous gift.

When built, the actual prototype will rise above the silos; whole communities are supposed live within it, and every citizen can view the relationships of planes and angles and surfaces from inside. In effect, they will be living within its creator's mind, observing, perhaps subjectively evaluating, how his intellect worked out the different problems presented by his imagination, his speculation. They would be impressed and enclosed by his concept, his premise, in the same way these playgoers, two thousand years ago, were held within the imperial vision of Rome no matter how they responded to the comedy before them. Our friend hoped to extrude himself by this jackstraw assembly that would impose a model of his soul, mathematically proved, upon this Illinois plain. It would be a sort of Hegelian proof of himself and much better than one formulated in concrete or stone because it would be continuously renewed, reborn, and worked out by the generations living within it.

Outside the window, the conical roofs of the grain silos had turned orange with the light fleeing west across the prairie toward a horizon that pulled the rail lines together into a single, luminous thread. Farm boys clustered outside the lighted window of a barbecue café. It was a scene out of Wright Morris, and we could have been in the presence of genius here in this room also. Our daughter had become attentive, quiet. Here in Autun, only this theatre, a couple of gates, and some rubble of the old wall remain of that Roman city. The grand vision has been pillaged and appropriated into later models of human ambition.

I clean up my area of the old theatre, get into the Ford, and continue my journey through one of these two last gates, now called

Port d'Arroux: two handsome arches for vehicles flanked by two smaller ones for pedestrians—those Romans thought of almost everything—and topped by a gallery of pilasters with Corinthian capitals. This imperial exit lends me a sense of well-being, amply nourished by the delicious chicken, cheese, bread, and wine. And so, with a bite of pear, I salute D980, my new course. Le Morvan has moved even closer to the road and looms on my left.

Had I followed the Arroux to its source, digressed just a little to the right on N81, I would have ended up at Dijon where M. F. K. Fisher and her beloved Al feasted some fifty years ago. The flavors of her essays fill me with a sweet sadness, for I had hoped to learn the taste of red Meursault, a Coq au Chambertin, with another also, but it was not to be. Once again, my transient nature has probably discouraged such companionship, but, in any event, I do not wish to dine alone in Dijon, so I have taken the road to the left, D980, to enter the valley of the Ternin River and the rugged embrace of the Morvan.

Famous for its forests and rocky terrain, its Charolais cattle and network of rivers, this area was also known in the nineteenth century for the quality of its wet nurses. My Michelin tells me that leasing her breasts was "one of the most profitable occupations for the Morvan woman," and her milk was in great demand by the bourgeois mothers of Paris who thought it improper to nurse their own babies. Some local entrepreneurs carried their product to Paris, while others stayed unbuttoned in their villages where little hungry mouths were brought to the local taps. Farmed out, as it were. Come to think of it, didn't Zola's *Nana* bring her unfortunate babe down here somewhere to be fed so as not to depreciate the charms of her own *nichons*?

So it could be said that I have put myself on a path between two gastronomical interests: to the right the romantic and delicious tables of Dijon, and on my left the rocky environs of more basic nourishment. But let's put aside the literary allusion to Fisher, with its sigh of self-pity, because this footnote on the bountiful bosoms of the Morvan has teased out another speculation. Perhaps I have taken this road as a metaphorical trip back to the tit that was abruptly popped from my mouth a half century ago. At least, as I drive this winding road, I take the opportunity to think about that rejection, to enjoy and even wallow in the anger I have lately begun to feel for that withdrawal of sustenance. Perhaps I should examine the village women of Chissy, up the road, for a font at which I may slake my frustrated thirst? Too late, of course.

But here are the facts. After one year of nursing me, my mother left me in Kansas City in the care of her parents and returned to my father in New York City. I lived with my grandparents until I was fourteen. Why this took place has never been satisfactorily explained, but thanks to the affection and loving care of Tom and Mollie Coyne, I don't believe the sudden cutoff of maternal nourishment damaged me very much. Interestingly, it never occurred to me that I had been abandoned until I began writing a family biography years later. So what's the problem?

For one thing, this unusual arrangement did put me on the road—maybe even on this narrow route through the eastern part of the Morvan. From the age of two I began to commute between Kansas City and New York, making the round-trip every summer by train or Greyhound bus and once on a Trans Western Airline's DC-3. On most of these trips, I traveled by myself in the care of a porter or a bus driver to be met by my mother or my grandparents at the terminus. So, I rolled back and forth through the eastern half of the United States, coasting through towns and cities to take out a brief citizenship, or, for a few passing seconds, join a family in a car as they waited at a crossing. "A rolling stone gathers no moss," my mother was fond of saying, and surely the credo seemed to work for her. Neither of us had read Sartre or Camus—neither Sartre nor Camus had written much to read at that point. My mother would never read them. This French road has suddenly changed its number.

The route has become D20. The resinous perfume of conifers envelops my senses. Most of Paris's Christmas trees are cut from these plantations, another local product exported to the urban market. The valley has begun to close in on me and my Ford, and the road begins to ascend. I have to downshift. Flecks of brilliant sunlight begin to dart from the roadside vegetation to dash themselves against the windshield. The distance I have just traveled in the last few kilometers, to Kansas City and back, and through decades and back, doesn't really surprise me. All memory, no matter the date of its manufacture, is preserved on the same shelf of the mind.

That particular weaning in Kansas City has probably given me a tramp's thirst for the unencumbered trek. For a period of more than ten years, I became an itinerant hack, driving from one campus to another to take up temporary appointments as a "visiting writer" (the title alone courts certain philosophical considerations). I told myself the purpose of this circuit riding was to relocate my identity, my self-esteem, and to keep my children's respect, independent of their mother's money. What lofty motives! But maybe it was only the stone set rolling around within me like a counterweight that propelled me away from home and a marriage, leaving behind my children and their affection though I may have sustained their respect. I put myself in transit—even on this road through the Morvan. Even in this essay.

But these gloomy thoughts are left below in the shadows of the river valley, for I come onto a high plateau in full sunlight as the road changes its number once again: D121. Here the pine forests are spotted with stands of ancient oak and beech, remnants of great forests that once stood here before they were logged and sent downriver to Paris for firewood. It is cooler as well as brighter, and Saulieu is just down the other side of this mesa. It's midafternoon, but I have done quite enough traveling for one day, and I decide to stop there. Its kitchens have made the place famous.

The old Paris–Lyon post road runs through the town and has become the well-traveled N6, one of the principal routes through central France since the seventeenth century. In fact, the name of my hotel is Le Poste. Napoleon is supposed to have spent the night here on his way back from Elbe before going on to his appointment at Waterloo. The hotel is an attractive construction of exposed timbers and whitewashed stucco, and the corridor to my room falls away to the right and creaks underfoot like the companionway of a great ship under sail. My room is small but charming and has a window that looks out over the inner courtyard where horses must have been stabled and where I have parked my little blue Ford. But the dining room has been decorated with a belle époque elegance that puts me off, and the prices seem a little inflated as well. I crave a simpler atmosphere for dinner; the day has been complicated enough.

My journal does not record how I spent the rest of the afternoon. I don't recall visiting the famous basilica of St. Andoche. I have no recollection of the local museum, which apparently features Saulieu's gastronomical history, nor did I pay my respects to the tomb of the animal sculptor François Pompon. I will remember passing by his famous bull in a park near the road out of town the next morning. Perhaps I took a nap.

Later I choose the Lion d'Or from the several restaurants along the rue Grillot. The neat handscript of its menu, posted beside the entrance, pricks my appetite. The careful formation of the characters and the words' forthright demeanor on the page make for an appealing implication of the chef's manner in the kitchen. Also, the prix fixe is within my budget.

Inside, the restaurant is quiet and almost bare of decoration. At several tables, diners are already meticulously at work, and there is little conversation. This is a serious place. Seated, I become aware of the large glass panes, like the show windows of an auto agency, that front the width of the dining room, and these have been closed to the traffic of the thoroughfare outside by oatmeal-colored drapes of a heavy material.

The woman who brought me to my table returns with a menu, a basket of bread, and a small plate of andouillettes as a complimentary starter. She is obviously in charge, but her manner suggests that she may have just risen from one of the other tables, interrupted her own meal with a favored guest in order to serve me; yet, I am to take my time, not feel pressed by any consideration for her. Such distractions from her own pleasures come with her responsibilities to her patrons—to be assumed, m'sieur. She is dressed as if she might have lectured somewhere on Descartes that afternoon. She wears a tailored skirt and jacket, a straw-colored blouse of silk with an agate broach at the throat. Her shoes are expensive looking, sturdy and polished. As I have been munching the crumbly saltiness of the little sausages, she has been waiting patiently for me to choose the wine.

When I look up from the menu, the expression on her face startles me. Madame has been worriedly observing me, concerned perhaps that I might come up with the wrong choice, that I would make a selection that would embarrass the whole dining room. Men would throw their napkins down in disgust, pushing back their chairs as their wives jump up trembling and affronted to push ahead of them, children wailing and still clutching a half-eaten tarte aux pommes—all of them storming out of the place, arms raised and indignation spewing from their well-sauced lips.

I ask for the Côte de Beaune-Joliette. Madame brightens—her "tres bien" rings with approval. An economical choice to be sure—but frugality is a virtue, and it is a vintage surely not unaware of its own subtleties. Her attitude has so favored me, and the other diners have reasonably resumed their solemn degustations. I order the rest of my meal: a soupe de lotte Tante Angela, fricassee canard au vinaigrette, a mixed green salad.

It is only then that I notice the immense mural beside me. It takes up one half of the dining room's inside wall and depicts a chaotic scene: a carriage has just arrived at an inn—perhaps at Le Poste down the street, where I stay. The artist is not primitive, but he has too faithfully reproduced every face and costume within this seventeenth-century context. Couples and relatives embrace and kiss. Children are lifted high and hugged. Dogs chase around the carriage's wheels and beneath the nervous hooves of horses reined in tight by grooms. Other boys hand down luggage from the coach. The innkeeper, his cheeks the size and color of crab apples, welcomes a stylish couple at the door. And in the center, like the star making her entrance, is a handsome woman who is attempting to manage voluminous skirts as she steps down from the carriage. The artists have given her a rather roguish mien. This might be Madame Sévigné, who is remembered in Saulieu for getting a little tipsy during a stopover. Had she already had a few in the carriage, sipped from a small flask to settle the stomach on a bumpy post road, or does that expectant look reflect her anticipation of something agreeable to knock down in the tavern? Did she include this event in any of her famous letters to her daughter? *My dear Francoise—Your generous nature will perhaps*

embrace your mother's folly here in Saulieu for which I have given
a statue in penance to the basilica of St. Andoche. Perhaps I could
write my daughter from Saulieu, ask her to embrace my folly. Or
has she become irretrievably serious in this estrangement? Is there
no level of fatuity in my behavior that can amuse her, persuade
her to love my clown attire?

But the soup has been served. Aunt Angela's way with eels is fragrant with sage and saffron and maybe thyme. The dish resembles
a tomatoless bouillabaisse and is thoroughly delicious. After Madame has circumspectly removed the empty bowl, I'm given a certain amount of time to contemplate what I have just enjoyed. The
wine in my glass has rounded another mellow dimension. Then
she's back with the main dish, which she presents with an offhand
pride. The rich brown sauce, enforced by Armagnac, glistens on
the crackly surface of the duck leg adorned with sprightly green
sprigs of watercress. The pungent meat pulls away from the bone
like silk. Have the walnuts been added to the green salad especially
to compliment the husky flavors of the canard, or are they a usual
flourish? The wine has darkened from ruby to garnet, deepening
its flowing accompaniment to the meal like a subdued scherzo.

These accumulated satisfactions give me appetite to find something good in my daughter's letter. Whatever course this discord
may take, she has at least confronted me, has strongly objected to
my imperial imposition of self upon her own image. She demands
self-definition and rejects my projection of who I think she is.
How many women, I wonder, have been unable to make such a
stand only to go through life in a continuous disagreement with
men—and consequent dissatisfaction with themselves—because
they never dissented with the original man in their lives? Our
literature, our soap operas—the soap operas that pass for our
literature—are driven by such melodramatic counterweights, and

the pattern becomes stuck in its own repetition. My mother never rebelled against her father's stern sergeant-major manner, then she sought and found a similar Augustus in my father, and only then did she come to her sense of self, striking out on her own and refashioning herself, but leaving me in order to do so. That first distancing created this lust I have for the solo trip—safety in solitude. And so on. For isn't this the ironic *casse en route* that in recent years, I have reinvented that initial abandonment by falling in love with young women who have yet to secure themselves and who must leave me to make their own images, find their own footing? Surely, this Côte de Beaune has properties Madame could never have imagined.

But there are important decisions to be made—should it be the *tarte aux poire* or *fromage*? She suggests, if only to close the stomach, a local cheese called Epoisses, and for reasons that would only greatly distress her, I am happy to place myself in her hands.

As if on cue, the bland consistency of music that has flowed through the restaurant from a discrete sound system has been strikingly interrupted. The indifferent envelopment of drapery and neat napery has been pushed aside by the crooning wail of a saxophone. It is a Toni Morrison saxophone, a tenor sax pulled down from the night sky and perhaps played by Stanley Turrentine to weave an American elegy of city nights, windows open on fire escapes as the loneliness of a lost love cools in its own sweat. I must be the only one in the room to hear this call; my fellow victualers continue their inexorable consumption. It's as if the soul, the jazz of America, has searched me out, found me at this table in Saulieu to impose its sentimental litany upon my wandering thoughts.

One face stands out in the mural, in fact he is looking just over my shoulder and meets my eye—the only figure to so engage the viewer. He is a village local, capped and booted, clay pipe in his mouth, and he has just returned from the hunt. He cradles a heavy fowling piece in one arm, a game bag hangs from one shoulder, and he holds a large rabbit by the ears. It looks as if he has just rounded the corner of the inn to come upon this busy arrival scene, and he looks at me with a bemused expression. What's all this fuss about, he seems to ask? This human jostle is rather droll, don't you think?

I've seen this fellow before in Italy, in frescoes of holy scenes—Old Testament barbarisms and awesome feats of levitation. Usually he stands in the corner of the painting and sometimes bears the features of the painter—once or twice in the persona of an animal, a horse or a sheep. It is a device to call attention to what's going on. It does not ask for an interpretation or impose an opinion, but only asks that we witness this human event. The hunter looking over my shoulder is saying, "See what's happening here. Here we all are." In transit, we pause for a little rest, step down from the day, careful of how we present ourselves, and have something to eat, a little wine, and perhaps write a letter or two at the end of this day in Burgundy.

Passing through Pittsburgh

The Greater Pittsburgh phone directory lists 191 numbers under the family name of *Coyne*, and there must be other households of that name that are not listed or who may not have a telephone. Not exactly in the same league with the Joneses, but yet a sizable Irish colony, which may explain why my grandfather showed up here around 1875 at the age of fifteen, his first stop on a trek toward a citizenship that always seemed to elude him.

Tom Coyne, his brothers, and one sister all immigrated together, having walked from their village of Leenane, west of Galway City, to Queenstown, or Cork, where they took the boat for America. Whispers in family archives suggest a melodramatic flight from British authorities due to the body of a priest being found pitchforked on the family sheep farm. This was the time of "the tithe," and the younger Coynes' father, Black Phillipe, was supposed to have had enough of the ecclesiastical rip-off, whether by the Roman Catholic Church or the Church of England. So, as the story goes, they were on the lam, and someone may have said, "You have cousins in Pittsburgh, Pennsylvania. They'll take you in." But the Coyne siblings all split up upon coming ashore in the New World, further suggesting they were running from something, and, in fact, when my grandfather made his only return to Ireland at the age of ninety, he tried to get a passport under an assumed name. He might still be wanted, he feared. Whatever the circumstances, he was the only one of that family to come to Pittsburgh, and he was vague about his time here in 1875. It seems he was only passing through.

Carnegie, McCandless, and Company had been founded by 1873, and the Edgar Thomson Steel Works in Braddock had already installed the first Bessemer. Frick's Coke empire was underway, and glass-making was a close second to steel as an industry in this boomtown where one could feel "the actual physical presence of power," to use the words of a contemporary *Wall Street Journal* article.

Tom Coyne must have breathed the power of the place, felt the heat and rhythm of its industry. The great number of steamboats and barges on the rivers probably impressed him, for they served the largest inland harbor of that time. He was fond of such assessments; the largest *this*, the greatest *that*, the most powerful *other*, maybe because he was a small man himself, wiry and resilient but with a Celtic fury in his eyes to compensate for his stature. After his army career, his life would be fitted to heavy machinery—locomotives, the great locks of the Panama Canal—engines to cross and move the earth and divert oceans. Along with the river vessels, the six railroads that focused on Pittsburgh must have firmly centered this fascination.

And in all probability he arrived in Pittsburgh by train, coming from Kings Point, Brooklyn, where he landed—this some twenty years before Ellis Island—to Philadelphia and then Pittsburgh. Just two years before, in 1873, the train trip from Philadelphia to Pittsburgh had been cut down from twenty-five hours to only twelve—what better proof to this young immigrant of the powerful society he thought he had joined. The place fired his sentience for human invention to a white-hot fervor that was never to cool.

Why didn't he stay? "The mill work was too much for me. I wasn't strong enough for it." But he was strong enough to break and handle cavalry horses only a couple of years later. Strong enough to construct railroads all through Mexico and Central America. In Ecuador he built and ran the railroad from Quito to Guayaquil—an arduous construction that crossed the Andes. In his seventies he was strong enough to disarm two muggers in Kansas City, to send them fleeing and to capture one when the man fell over a fireplug. When the police showed up, they found Tom Coyne kicking the thief's behind. He had to be restrained. So it wasn't that he was weak or fragile, but for some other reason he got back on another train after a year or two in Pittsburgh and headed west. He was a Connemara lad and perhaps there were aspects to Pittsburgh, with all its industrial wonder, that were too much for him. Or not enough.

Some years later I am going by train in the opposite direction, and I am eight years old. My mother and I have taken a Missouri-Central from Kansas City to Chicago where we changed to a Pullman sleeper on the Pennsylvania Railroad. The next morning my father will meet us at the Pennsylvania Station in New York, and we taxi across town to Grand Central where we get on a train of the New York Central's Harlem Division that will take us, on a road bed laid down in 1852, to a small town near a rented farm house in Columbia County. The whole trip will take the better part of two days and a night. It is a summer pilgrimage I was to make many times to fulfill my parents' peculiar concept of a family, for my grandparents kept me nine months of the year. But that's another digression.

This particular trip east occasioned my first look at Pittsburgh, and it was a sleepy look from beneath the blind of my Pullman berth's window, but it was a sight that burned into my remembrance. Midnight or early morning, the train's scheduled arrival in

Pittsburgh is unknown to me, but it is pitch dark. Some change in the train's rhythm has awakened me. I snuggle down in the cozy cave of my upper berth—no bed linen will ever match the crisp luxury of Pullman sheets; they had the cool freshness of a fine memory.

Nor, if I may switch onto a little sidetrack, has the special effect of train travel been matched by any other form—something's been lost. Train travel permits a passenger to encounter others in a different space, poses a relativity between object and viewer which Einstein fully appreciated. These days we mostly travel cut off from the world we traverse, only our destination and arrival time are defined. But to pass by train through a countryside, to take up temporary residence in another place, and to intersect, however briefly, with other lives waiting patiently at a road crossing, that particular human experience has been all but lost, and I think the human imagination, without this free association, has been impoverished.

But here I am, entering Pittsburgh at eight years of age on a Pennsylvania Pullman to New York City, coming up the Ohio River with McKees Rocks on the right, then into that cut through West Park, and across the Allegheny at 11th Street into Daniel Burnham's gorgeous terminal, erected to replace the old depot that was burned down during the 1877 railroad riots. The riots would have occurred a couple of years after Tom Coyne came to town.

I raise the window blind and, still drugged with sleep, look out on a scene that Turner could have painted. Violent explosions of color, of whiteness. Billowing clouds of fire blossom from the dark to metastasize into orange and scarlet plumes. The sun is coming apart. I am terrified and fascinated all at once, as it is always awesome to look into the center of power. My mind's camera was permanently marked with this image of the mills turning common ore into iron and steel, making something new out of the ordinary—an immense, catastrophic breakdown and reintegration.

Tom Coyne must have had a similar view. The particle residue of coal fires clogged the air, not just from the mills but from the city's fireplace grates. Perhaps my grandfather warmed himself on cold winter mornings at one of these narrow grates, let's say, staying with a Coyne cousin. He never said, so I am free to wonder. Maybe he didn't hit it off with the relatives—personal relationships were not his forte—so he might have rented a bed in one of the many rooming houses that boarded single men, mill hands, perhaps in one of the row houses of my neighborhood on the North Side in which the floor planks of yellow pine still show the old nail holes that marked off those cramped corners that transformed a normal-sized living room into a crowded dormitory.

Surely, he might have thought, this was a paltry citizenship he had exchanged for the fresh air of Connemara, the dew of Galway still upon him. For these grimy alleys, he had left clear streams where trout fought for a place on the hook. For this gritty domain, he had turned away from the long vista of Killary Bay where salmon entered to spawn and Viking ships had once ghosted on a westerly breeze. It may have been this mystical perspective that pulled him away from Pittsburgh, and not the hard work, for his whole life was one of hard work. It would be too clever a hindsight to suggest that he objected to being separated from the product made by his hard work, and with borrowed tools at that, or that he felt himself made expendable—dross to be burned out to make more efficient fuel. Those ideas were around then, of course, but he never thought that way. No, I think those mystical images he carried from Ireland pulled him away. He tried to duplicate them on the coulees of Montana, in the jungles of Central America, and the heights of the Andes. Then there were those riots of 1877.

The management of the Pennsylvania Railroad, the same company that brought him and me through Pittsburgh at different times, had decided to do a little downsizing in 1877. Trainmen's salaries were to be cut 10 percent; moreover, freight train lengths were to be doubled, thereby reducing the number of jobs as well. The city rebelled. Burghers blocked the tracks. Mayor McCarthy refused to call in the police, and the members of the local state militia would not raise arms against their neighbors. Under pressure from the railroad company, Governor John Frederick Hartranft called up the militia quartered in Philadelphia, and after arriving by train, these men assembled, confronted the citizenry, and on July 21 fired into a crowd, killing twenty people. All hell broke loose. The mob drove the troops out of Pittsburgh. Over a thousand freight cars were demolished, and nearly 150 locomotives were destroyed. Dozens of downtown buildings, including the depot, were burned to the ground. The city was brought to a halt, to the edge of total anarchy, and it was the most violent uprising in America since the Civil War, not to be equaled until the riots of the 1960s. I can understand how it discouraged my grandfather. How was this oppression of a citizenry any different from the situation he had just left? Exchange the Pennsylvania Railroad's board of directors with Queen Victoria's cabinet, and it looked like the same sort of tyranny he had learned to hate at his father's knee. It had been waiting for him here in Pittsburgh. And the air was bad, too.

Something else to conjure: almost exactly a year before, on July 4, 1876, George Armstrong Custer led the Seventh Cavalry to its destruction on the banks of the Little Bighorn River. The battle had made all the papers. The stupidity of Custer's foray was glossed over by the glory of his death, for his opponents this time around were not the old men, women, and children slaughtered at Washita and Sand Creek, but were—as my grandfather was to say later—"the greatest light horse cavalry ever to go into battle." So it was something like a fair fight, and in the clean, open air as well. My grandfather might even have been cheered by the Sioux victory; the underdog had won this time, and though he was to spend five years in the U.S. Cavalry, his sympathies were always with the Indians. The irony was not lost on him that to gain his own citizenship, he had to suppress and diminish the citizenship of others. This awful paradox would sometimes make him weep.

So he left Pittsburgh. "I worked on the railroad," he would say when asked how he got to California, and that was all he would say. The Irish laid a lot of track, going east to west, as the Chinese did from west to east. Unskilled labor, such as a mill worker, was about all that was available to him in a society that discretely placed signs in its windows: *No Irish Need Apply*. "Sometimes I was called a white nigra," he told me once, and the confusion still welled up in his pale-blue eyes. Yes, the comparison offended him, but also he was outraged that men, African or Celt, should be put into such an equation at all. In San Francisco he enlisted in the U.S. Cavalry at the presidium: five years of service would give him citizenship, at least on paper, and these were to be "the happiest days of my life." He was assigned to the Yellowstone whose trout-packed streams along with the clean air reminded him of Connemara. He also witnessed the American Indians' harmony with nature, and their way of life would become a lifelong paradigm.

But what looks smooth to me this morning on Monterey Street was actually a disjointed record. We make such narratives to iron out the discontinuity of our lives, give tumbled events a cause and effect—even a reason they may not have possessed. The endeavor comforts us as it helps us believe that we were, in some way, in charge of the past when it was happening—a condescension as much as a folly—though this behavior might explain the myopic affection we have for the past, worked into sweet nostalgia like a piece of leather until it is soft and supple to our self-appraisals. Worked on until past events come out right. We prefer unity in these revisions, everything under one roof so to speak, the piece-meal configurations of the original smoothed over. Card players illustrated by Norman Rockwell pleasure this nostalgia—the same game pictured by Cezanne can scare the hell out of us.

So, I admit to a certain lack of control over this material, and merely to put the different parts of my life, my grandfather's life, and Pittsburgh into a pretty cohesion will only be my arbitrary arrangement of the bits and pieces. The particles themselves will remain unaltered and unexplained and the inquiry unoccasioned—an idle amusement and nothing more.

However, two years after my first passage through Pittsburgh, I came through once again, but this time by plane. My grandfather gave me a roundtrip ticket to join my parents via a Trans Western Airlines DC-3, which stopped to refuel in Chicago and Pittsburgh. The flight took over six hours, about the same time it took Tom Coyne to go from Philadelphia to Pittsburgh, and I mention this commonplace only to recall his exultation when I became part of this proof of modernity, a passenger on this demonstration of human invention. My grandmother was more of a traditionalist and was apprehensive of all gadgets, especially those that lifted a person several thousand feet into the air. "I can see his little legs dangling through the clouds," she said worriedly.

I enjoyed the trip, pampered by the stewardess with extra helpings of chocolate cake and chewing gum, but the time spent on the ground in Pittsburgh draws a blank. Unlike that other early morning passage, I can call up from memory no views of the steel mills, no clouds of fire and smoke, not even a trace of the rivers' fork. Moreover, we landed far outside of town at the old airport.

The plane's altitude and flight path separated me from these city marks, so my memory is left holding an empty contour, but I was distanced from more than a place.

Back on the ground of this Pittsburgh where I live, a similar separation from place, from a past meant to nourish the present, has been happening here and in all American cities during the last half of this century. It goes by such names as "urban renewal" and "cultural renaissance," and it is a process born of the suburban mentality that has always lived outside a city's limits and is uncomfortable within the rough edges of its neighborhoods. So bulldozers are called in to smooth the awkward edifices of the past; selected artifacts are installed in museums to be viewed safely on weekends.

My own neighborhood had been a part of Allegheny City, an independent urban entity across the Allegheny River from downtown Pittsburgh. Fifty years ago, the five hundred buildings of this commercial center were torn down and replaced by a mall—that vulgar pastoral of suburban zeal. Today, this mall is all but empty; a derelict of corrupt planning because the local populace had been isolated by its very construction, separated from their natural thoroughfares and haunts. Most of these places have been obliterated and major streets truncated.

To build the Civic Arena, home of the Pittsburgh Penguins, fifteen hundred African American families were made refugees in their own city and neighborhood. Perhaps there is a connection between this displacement and a statistic that puts this city at the top of the list for having the greatest number of impoverished African American families. Cut off the circulation in a hand and it becomes numb, useless, and it is the same with a neighborhood. Cut off the flow of its inborn traffic and its citizenry is diminished. The place rots. Perhaps city people should be wary of suburbanites seeking, if not bearing, culture.

Lately, a so-called Cultural District has been marked off in the center of the city and designed for attractions that will lure culture hounds from the glens of Fox Chapel and Sewickley. But how can culture be segregated, and is it wise to do so? Culture is diminished when set apart from the community that is supposed to inspire it, indeed, from which its own inspiration is drawn. It becomes legal and bland. This current undertaking is merely another mall that will market the national chains of entertainment enterprises: fuzzy reproductions of Broadway boilerplate and the weary appearances of celebrity artistes on the road. It is more than a passing irony that the "renewed" area previously hosted the city's prostitutes and porno dens, agents of another kind of veneration that was also set apart from the community. But vice has always been segregated, and now, in Pittsburgh, it seems to be culture's turn. At the same time, I would guess that in the neighborhood bars of Bloomfield, Homewood, and the South Side, more genuine, spontaneous culture (neighborhood myths and local heroes remembered) is celebrated on any night of the week than in a whole season of imported attractions in the glittering halls downtown.

Tom Coyne, in his quest for citizenship, wanted to join the power of Pittsburgh. He wanted to contribute his energy and invention to that power, but he had to move on because he found the power was exclusive, misdirected, and made harmful to the very people it was supposed to enhance and amplify. My search for identity is neither as desperate nor as direct; after all, I am second generation and can afford to loaf a little on the banks of these three rivers. But I am no less mindful of the struggle for identity, for a place on this river delta; so, in the temporal coincidence some call history, Tom Coyne and I are merely passing through.

Three Places
in Ohio

A little more than midway through my journey, I prepare to descend from the twentieth floor of Pittsburgh's sparkling Gateway Center, where I have just met with a lawyer to make my last will and testament. The elegant offices of his firm offer a comfort so deeply carpeted as to soothe the most anxious footfall, so I enter the elevator confident that my last good intentions are in good hands. Just as the elevator doors slide closed, another man slips through.

He appears to be a senior partner. Well-tailored and at ease with himself, he looks at me sideways and smiles. "What are you doing for the Fourth?" he asks as we begin to descend.

Well, as a matter of fact, my wife's birthday falls a few days after the holiday—and on a weekend this year—and I have planned a little excursion, a surprise trip to East Liverpool, Ohio, about an hour's drive from Pittsburgh, just across the Ohio River.

"It's only part of the festivities," I hasten to tell him, "but there's a small café there, Brickers, where we had a marvelous breakfast a few years ago. Grits and ham gravy, wonderful home fries, eggs fried in butter, and biscuits. Strong coffee. Like an old-time place." My companion has been nodding knowingly. Despite his cosmopolitan manner and attire, he is clearly a man of solid tastes.

"Then you should drive south from there," he tells me as we near the ground floor. "Take Route 7 along the river to a small place called Fly. There's a restaurant there on the river bank that serves wonderful pie." The doors open smoothly, and he disappears into the milling lobby.

So, go to Fly for pie. It must be a message sent to me from some divinity on high, at least from the twentieth floor, and I am particularly receptive to such oracular recommendations since for the past hour the subject on the stylish conference table upstairs has been my death. Nor is this the first time I have visited these legal chambers under the threat of death.

A few years ago an associate began to make abusive phone calls to me, and in one of these he even threatened to kill me. Certainly, his behavior is an extreme example of the puny power struggles familiar to all institutions, but I took him seriously; moreover, the man's maniacal jealousy began to affect my home life. My wife heard one of his messages on our answering machine and was unable to sleep that night. So I took my complaints, along with one of these phone messages my wannabe assassin obligingly left behind on tape, to a lawyer of this firm. He took the attacks seriously, too, for they constituted, according to him, "harassment with the intention to cause emotional harm," a statute upheld by the Supreme Court, and he notified my assailant of this finding, adding that legal action would be taken if he continued his malicious behavior.

The lawyer's letter has not quelled the man's vicious anger, enwrapped in a sanctimonious manner so finely developed as to suggest he waits to fill a vacancy in the Holy Trinity—as Mark Twain would observe—but I have been able to answer the phone without anticipating his malevolent harangue.

But every itinerary includes a death threat, and we must learn to live with the knowledge of this stopover, even to devise strategies to give some dimension to its immeasurable closure. And what better strategy on this bright July weekend but to go to East Liverpool, Ohio, and to Brickers Cafeteria and Deli for a late breakfast.

East Liverpool is a small city of about fourteen thousand people that has come to be known as the "pottery capital of the world." Soon after the area was surveyed as part of the Northwest Territory, the local soil was discovered to be rich in a clay that made high-quality ceramic products. By the end of the nineteenth century a thriving industry turned out tableware and other china articles, and the amount of money made from clay pots can be estimated from the elaborate façades of Victorian mansions that line the side streets of East Liverpool today. Several companies continue the trade, including the ubiquitous Fiestaware, and the same natural resource supports other firms that make clay products for the electronic and communication industries.

In 1934 the little town on the Ohio River achieved a momentary national notoriety when the rural hoodlum "Pretty Boy" Floyd was gunned down by G-men in a nearby cornfield. His bullet-riddled body was put on display in a local funeral home to attract thousands of Depression-era mourners who stood in long lines to pay tribute to this hero who had dared attack the banks that had ruined them. For some reason, as I write these words, a picture forms in my mind of J. Edgar Hoover, clutching a Thomson submachine gun to his immaculate pinstripe and wearing a grim look and a snap-brim fedora. I wonder if he had been in that cornfield.

But it is Brickers Cafeteria and Deli ("Home-Cooked Food") that brings us to East Liverpool this morning, and to pass into its aroma is to enter a realm of orderly satisfaction. Of life. The

delicatessen is in the front of the establishment, and it is not particularly unique. But at the rear and slightly to the right lies the
grill and small cafeteria, and here motherly and even grandmo-
therly women wearing crisp blue smocks over their dresses cook
and serve the delicacies that make this unpretentious place one of
the more noteworthy culinary haunts along the Ohio River.

At the grill a customer may order eggs in any form, with or
without pancakes. Grits, corned-beef hash, gravies from red-eye
up through the more subtle whites, side orders of various meats,
including homemade sausage, and of course—home fries. The
home fries have been neatly pushed to the back of the cook top
so that their innate goodness is slowly teased to the surface by the
continuous heat. These are not the mechanically cut spuds found
on the usual grill, whose conformity of size and shape discourages
the palate even before the first forkful. The home fries at Brickers
are a tumbled, jolly pile of tubers, chopped indiscriminately into
a countless profusion of shapes and sizes. The smaller nuggets have
been basted in bacon grease to a charred crunchiness that when
taken in the mouth with a larger, more pliant portion can flood
the darkest introspection with undeniable light. "Death is not
present here," Epicurus might say, "so it should not concern us."

The lady at the grill turns pancakes in one corner of the surface
and rolls sausages in another. Two eggs cook sunny side up in a
third area. "So her water broke this morning," she tells a colleague
who holds plates of steaming grits, "and I said to him, 'what did
the doctor say?' and he says, 'any time today.' Oh, I have to go
through that again." Kathleen has tarried at this station, transfixed
by the possibilities sizzling before her, while I move on to the small
cafeteria-style tray railing. It is only about six feet long and passes
before a case stocked with freshly baked muffins, sticky buns, pies,
and popovers. I am trying to be a man of restraint, the secrets and
the delights that await us downriver in Fly abetting my self-control.

But then a hand-scrawled card on the counter announces the morning special to be "sausage gravy on biscuit." I must have it.

I know something about gravy and what makes good gravy. I was once married to a woman from West Virginia who is probably one of the great gravy makers of all time. Moreover my grandmother's Sunday gravy from roast chicken drippings yet pools in my memory in all its brown luxuriance. My old friend Bill Humphrey often bragged of the gravy cooked up in his East Texas childhood, so it seems to me that the great gravies in American cuisine all have been stirred on southern stovetops. "Poor-folk food," Bill used to say appreciatively as his wife, Dorothy, blended the mixture over a moderate flame with the same patient respect she gave to risotto or polenta—two supreme concoctions, incidentally, that share similar humble origins.

To be ignorant of gravy and its making is to be ignorant of the basic ingredients of life and how to appreciate that life. Flour and grease, some water, and a little flavoring—these ordinary elements, when combined rightly, produce an extraordinary nostrum that can appease almost any human hunger, alleviate almost any anxiety. Almost.

We have been waiting for our orders as we sip coffee ("55 cents—15 cents refills") in one of the plain, plastic-covered booths in the dining area. Behind us, in several booths near the exit, is a small legislature of older men, the shadow government to be found in small towns like East Liverpool. They drink coffee and smoke and talk and then drink more coffee—a regular rotation to and from the coffee urn at the cashier's station, which probably explains the charge for refills.

But our dishes have been served by another one of the women in a blue smock, and I wonder if they may belong to some sort of local guild, perhaps some older and wiser society of vestals sworn to minister to homely needs. Kathleen looks past her selection of eggs, bacon, home fries, and toast to my rather bland-looking plate of sausage gravy and biscuit. How deceptive the prosaic can be in nature and human affairs—how eccentricities and motivations are often unappreciated, and so it is with sausage gravy. But I'm not about to bring up this reflection, for she is already engaged with her breakfast. And so am I.

The moment my fork cuts through the crusty texture of the large biscuit, I know that all of my worldly concerns must lift with the first forkful. The flaky pastry pulls apart lingeringly to leave doughy pockets nuzzled by the smooth hotness of gravy. Ah, the gravy.

It is thick and runs silkily on the tongue, with a consistency redolent of fresh pepper and sharpened by salt. Chunks of sausage wallow and roll in this purity as the gravy spreads over the biscuit and the entire plate. The sausage is of the wet kind, in bulk, though link sausages are common in other versions, but this sausage before me is an immediate delight. Small satchels of the sweet meat are scattered abundantly through the white hotness to give the mixture its delicious flavor. The Brickers's brand of sausage is savored with the usual sage and marjoram, but there is a perfume-like flavor I cannot identify. Perhaps it is nutmeg. Perhaps it is ambrosia.

Since we cannot outlive the gods, we may try to out-eat them. Funeral feasts are common to every culture; in every rural community the tables of the bereaved creak beneath covered dishes, pots of stews, and platters of cooked meats and fowl. Food seems to be the way we challenge death or the threat of death. If we cannot have the last laugh, we can at least have a last good meal. I wonder if the citizens of East Liverpool put on their best bibs for Charles Arthur Floyd, who had just turned thirty in 1934.

South of East Liverpool, the Ohio River resembles the Rhone River around Valence where that valley narrows as N86 follows the West Bank to give a rolling panorama of an ageless landscape with abrupt hillsides. On Route 7, Kathleen and I can look to our left across the Ohio River to West Virginia. Steep cliffs tower above us, and both landfalls are lushly green in this July light. She has been only mildly curious as to why we are continuing our morning's drive, going on from Brickers toward an unannounced destination rather than returning to Pittsburgh. My promise of more birthday celebrations down the road has amused her, for she knows of my penchant to keep a festival's lights burning for as long as possible. I have kept secret the pie in Fly, but it is not the only secret I carry down Route 7 on this beautiful day by the Ohio River.

Just a day before our trip, and oddly only a week after I made my will, my doctor tells me that my latest blood test suggests that I have prostate cancer. My PSA count has jumped wildly over the mark that the medical profession has determined to be the borderline of that forbidding area, but it is a slow-moving disease, he assures me. "Something else will probably get you before it does."

I take the news calmly, possibly because before every visit to his office I have imagined this scene. His announcement and my response are like a moment we have both rehearsed, and we are letter-perfect. We know our lines. My mind is pulling back for a wider view, and I make some quick calculations based on my score. I've had a pretty good time of it; been lucky in love and career and haven't committed too many shameful acts on paper or in person. But, already?

He's been telling me that the next step would be a series of procedures that will probe my prostate gland and take a biopsy. If those findings are positive, as the blood test has indicated they may be, then some form of radiation therapy will be used. Yes, there may be some unpleasant side effects of the therapy such as impotency, but then he cheerfully reminds me of the fortuitous rise of Viagra. But he is of a conservative nature and does not rush decisions or treatments, and he wants me to have a second blood test in four months' time before all of the above is done.

So, it is this wait-and-see attitude, his reserving of a final opinion, that keeps me from telling Kathleen. She sits beside me, happily accompanying the show tunes we have brought on tape in her wonderfully sharp register. Later, she will be angry with me for not telling her and will accuse me of acting like a controlling male, but what was I supposed to say? "Happy Birthday, Darling, the doctor says I have prostate cancer." No, as I savor the two of us making this brilliant passage along the Ohio River, I am thinking that I give the both of us this day, give us Brickers Cafeteria and Deli, with the pie in Fly yet to come. It is a birthday gift for both of us.

Mammoth coal-fed power plants have appeared on both sides of the river. These faceless Goliaths with their slants of chutes angled above them look unattended and seem to process their fuel into electric power without anyone around to monitor the results, as if the men who threw the switches had also transformed themselves into invisible energy, leaving behind their polished pick-ups in the parking lot. At Empire we pass the dam and locks that control the river's flood stages while permitting a busy passage of tugs and barges, private craft, and the ornate reconstructions of large paddle wheelers bringing tourists to Pittsburgh or returning them to St. Louis and New Orleans.

At Steubenville, Route 7 has been renamed Dean Martin Boulevard to commemorate the singer's birthplace and where he came of age in local boxing rings, but on the other side of the city limits, the highway abruptly reverts to Route 7 as if none of that had ever happened. Farther down the road at Martin's Ferry, a modest marker renames the road once again, but as the Lou Groza Highway. I tell Kathleen about Lou "The Toe" Groza, the Hall of Fame place-kicker for the Cleveland Browns whose uncanny foot put 1,608 points on the scoreboard. But during that brief biography we have already passed through Martin's Ferry, and Route 7 has reclaimed its ordinary numerical identity. At this point in the journey it would be easy to craft an irony on transient celebrity—these sections of road so vainly renamed—but my fellow Burgher Warhol has already given a time limit to this distance that my odometer has routinely registered. West Virginia lies just ahead. Fly is not much farther and the river continues beside us unchanged.

Wheeling is an important manufacturing and commercial hub and is also a crossroad for U.S. Highway 70, the intercontinental highway that runs east and west along the beam of the United States. We are driving south, so we pass under it and at right angles to the overpass of this super highway, intersecting it but not exactly connecting either. I have made many journeys in many different cars on this road above us, driving west and back to take exits along its route to joy and venture, turning off into self-confidence and renewal—and all those other settlements it had been my good fortune to find along the way.

For as Kathleen sings beside me, I have been going over my accounts, adding up the work and pleasures of this life that has just been given its notice. My mind has turned in a sentimental basting to review my history, to spoon sweet memories over my noble acts. I stir together dollops of my generous behavior with sour portions of betrayal, everything folded into those times my inherent virtue had gone unrecognized. It's a tasty dish I set before myself on Route 7.

The dead ask only to be remembered, as Hamlet's father kept

saying over and over, but that poor ghost also wanted revenge, even if it meant driving his son to madness. And after all, are not last wills sometimes used by the dead to punish the living for simply living, documents drafted to get even with survivors for some wounding, some indifference suffered when they all breathed the same atmosphere? Moreover, a will is often a threat compounded beneath the threat of the ultimate threat, but I take pride—following the Ohio River—that the will I have just made has been drawn with love and affection. But other characters have begun to appear at the side of the road, spectral hitchhikers with their hands out and most with a finger up. They must be dealt with.

Dante's exile from Florence spurred his masterpiece, a magnificent act of revenge in which he consigned all those who had abused him to terza rimas of hell. Why shouldn't I do the same? Something not so fancy perhaps, but just as satisfying. The editors who have spurned and abandoned me, the feckless agents, the hustlers and gunsels of the writing game, a cowardly critic or two, ambition-crazed careerists, dishonest publishers, a former brother-in-law, one or two old classmates. The list seems endless, and we have only reached Powhatan Point! Let me not forget my half-brother, who questioned my legitimacy. And the thief who stole my father's cufflinks from my cold-water flat in New York the winter of 1952. Let's see, who else? A very large pool of fire for all those who have lied to me or told lies about me—and in a hot tub all to himself will be the man who has so abused me lately. But here's a chance to show charity—to show my good nature—for I will consign this fellow to a moderate temperature, a mediocre flame as befits his character. A slow cooker.

"Slow down," Kathleen warns me. "Why are you driving so fast? You are driving too fast."

And she's right. I am going too fast over this part of Route

7, which has just lost two of its lanes and has become a pleasant and even prettier two-lane highway. We have come nearly seventy miles from East Liverpool, and I look for signs of Fly. The Wayne National Forest has just appeared on our right, and its dense stands of black pine soothe me. On the river a tugboat pushes a string of empty barges north, and the day has become very warm.

One must look closely at Fly, Ohio, because there is not much to see. A filling station, two or three houses, a country saloon, and a restaurant called The Riverview. We have driven a hundred miles from East Liverpool, so when I pull into the parking lot of the Riverview, my wife is ready to agree. "It's time for a little pie," I tell her, and she nods.

Inside, booths are set around the knotty pine walls, and large windows overlook the river and the landing of a small ferry that takes travelers back and forth to Sistersville, West Virginia. This service has been operating since 1817, and the current craft is a small paddle wheeler that can take up to three cars. Above the middle counter of the restaurant a blackboard lists the day's pies. Every morning at six o'clock, a woman comes in and goes to the kitchen to bake six pies on weekdays and more on Sundays. Here are today's choices: peach, apple, blueberry, coconut custard, lemon meringue, and pumpkin. Another chalked menu announces the plats du jour: baked steak, salmon cakes, rolled cabbage.

My grandmother made salmon cakes on Fridays; canned salmon was cheap during the Depression. The contents of two cans would be mashed together with breadcrumbs, an egg, salt, pepper, and chopped celery leaves. The mass was divided and shaped into patties that were fried in Crisco and a bit of butter until the edges were crisp. Each patty received a spoonful of white sauce pebbled with fragments of hardboiled eggs and seasoned with paprika. Sometimes she would push the whole mixture into one large loaf with thin slices of lemon on top and then bake it to be served with the sauce in an ironstone boat on the side.

"What's that?" my grandfather would always ask, leaning low to peer at the serving platter as if the thing on it was the carcass of a varmint that had become trapped in the rosebushes.

"That's a salmon loaf, Tom," my grandmother would reply wearily.

"A salmon loaf," he would say in wonder. "Well, I'll be damned." And he would pick up the carving knife and fork and do his duty.

Kathleen is saying that the apple pie at the Riverview is very good but does not compare with her mother's. My piece of peach pie has been very satisfying. The crust has been on the short side, crumbly and not too sugared, and the peaches seem fresh. In both pies, there is no suggestion of cornstarch to thicken the filling, and generous portions of fruit fill the space.

What better way to celebrate these treats than to take the ferry across the Ohio River to Sistersville, West Virginia? The craft has been designed to take its lading from either side so as to allow the paddle wheel at the stern room for steerage. We are the only car on this trip. Several wooden picnic tables and benches have been set up on one section of the deck, and the wheelhouse stands high above. It's a two-man operation; the guy who has shown us where to park also closes the gate as the fellow above, his hands resting on the large wheel, looks down on us. Life on the Ohio.

With no ceremony, we have backed off from the riverbank and have turned toward midstream. Kathleen and I embrace in the sun's warmth and kiss as the river's current pulls at the little ferry. Crossing a river has mythical soundings in song and lore, and this particular passage has special meaning for me on this day in July. A school of black bass feeds just ahead, and one breaks surface to leap triumphantly into the air. Looking south, the river flows indolently, a strip of mirror in the light and framed by the green midsummer vegetation along its banks.

We are at midpoint, and this is the place by all the rules of narrative—if only those—that I should tell Kathleen about the test results. The story could almost write itself—the synthesis of place and destiny, the couple departing one bank to arrive at the other in different circumstances. But I want nothing to change this day, this being with her—nothing to puncture this radiant capsule of time.

As its name suggests, Sistersville was founded by two sisters, the daughters of an early settler. Oil was discovered here in the late nineteenth century to boom the town into a gushing prosperity for a couple of decades with all the banks, trolley lines, and whore houses a citizen could desire. The village we drive into from the ferry landing today is a sleepy river community with a two-block commercial center where store clerks talk desperately to strangers and a host of antique stores, heavy with patchouli, offer the remnants and cracked vessels of a fabled past. We have turned back toward Pittsburgh, my secret still shamefully hidden.

By August, my secret still hidden, my appetite is sharpened by the appearance of the Marietta tomato in local markets. These fruits from this southern Ohio community are deep red, with a plumpness that beguiles the most casual feel, and are not in the same crate with the dismal produce from Mexico and California. They are like the tomatoes my grandfather used to grow in our backyard in Kansas City and which gave new meaning to Wonder Bread.

WONDER BREAD TOMATO SANDWICH
(With Marietta tomatoes)

2 slices of fresh Wonder Bread—must be sticky, fresh
1 thick slab of Marietta tomato
1 thin slice of red onion
   Mayonnaise, salt, and pepper

Slather ample amounts of mayonnaise on both pieces of
bread. Place onion, then tomato on one slice. Salt and
pepper to taste. Then, place second slice over first and
press edges of bread together—all the way around to make
a strong seal. Then, bite into this pocket of goodness. . .

Marietta, Ohio, is 135 miles south of East Liverpool and inland
from the river as Route 7 turns west. The tomatoes in the Pittsburgh markets have reminded me that we stopped at a town restaurant in Marietta several years ago that served a prime example
of that classic of all classic dishes—a hot chicken sandwich with
gravy and mashed potatoes. The tang of that gravy over the suc-
culent slices of breast on spongy white bread has been kept warm
in the back of my memory ever since. I must have this dish once
more, to round out this pilgrimage the cicerone in the elevator
set me on last month.

The rails of old trolley lines yet limn the streets of downtown
Marietta, and the pink limestone courthouse holds down one
corner of the main intersection. This structure boasts an all-pur-
pose architecture. The first floor is a rough Romanesque that is
surmounted by a Palladian temple front, and a Sienese bell tower
tops both. The people here speak with a pleasant drawl, Kentucky
and West Virginia just across the Ohio River, and I feel very much
at home. But I cannot remember the name of the restaurant or
where it was located.

Mexican and Asian restaurants seem to be thriving, as are several fern bars and coffee spots. One place has a mammoth popcorn maker in its window with a candy counter behind. I peer through other windows, but nothing resembles the pleasant, narrow restaurant that had booths along one wall, a counter and cook area opposite. I can taste that gravy, and my mouth is watering.

At a newsstand, a woman directs me back to the place with the popcorn maker, The First Settler. I had asked for "the place that serves hot chicken sandwiches." The large machine in the window had obscured the booths in the rear, and I feel vindicated when I enter and my nose prickles with the heavy aroma of chicken gravy. Everything is as I remember it. I take one of the booths. Two men at the counter drink coffee and talk loudly of backhoes. Several booths down, a very old lady carefully spoons soup into her mouth, looking blankly around after each swallow as if trying to determine the flavor.

We are the only customers in the booths served by a pleasant young woman wearing a ruffled apron over slacks and a sweater. Two women work behind the counter: one at the stove and steam table and the other to serve. The server has just refilled the coffee cups of the two men, one of whom has just said something to her that makes her laugh a little—after she thinks about it.

Meanwhile, the waitress has brought me a menu and a glass of water. I don't open the menu; I know what I want. "I'll have that hot chicken sandwich with mashed potatoes and gravy," I tell her. She looks troubled.

"We have deep-fried chicken. We don't have a hot chicken sandwich, " she says.

"You used to have it."

Her eyes shift nervously. "Mary Anne," she cries, and the woman at the griddle looks our way. She checks the items cooking and walks toward us, a worried look on her face. I could be a traveler making an untoward advance on her younger colleague, an oaf without the savoir fair of the local at the counter.

Circumspectly, I describe the dish I ate in this very spot, perhaps this very same booth, just a few years back. She looks dubious. I want to get up and leave. But maybe this disappointment is meant to prepare me for all the last meals to come—that I must eat whatever they might be. We must accept what can be put together at the last moment, thrown together from whatever is on hand. In fact, the older woman is offering me just such an improvisation.

"I can take some of that deep fried and lie it on some bread and put gravy over."

"And mashed potatoes?"

She smiles. "Sure mashed potatoes, too."

When the young waitress returns with this spontaneous creation, she is beaming, and I feel a little like Robinson Crusoe making a new life out of salvage. Moreover, in this one desperate stroke, I have probably enlarged the menu of the First Settler, and that could be something of a legacy. She has paused after putting the plate before me, as if to share in the appreciation of what we have created. Then she leaves me to my pleasure.

The gravy that spills over the sandwich and settles into the cone of mashed potatoes is a chicken-leg yellow and with an intense flavor on the salty side. The slices of chicken beneath are crunchy on the edges and not the tender slices of meat I have craved. The white bread is acceptable and the mashed potatoes smoothly made. It's a filling meal. I've been given a small salad, and the several chunks of tomato lying in shavings of iceberg lettuce quickly interest me. But they are tasteless pulps. Where is the Marietta tomato?

"We import the tomatoes," the cook tells me as I pay the bill. In fact, she seems unaware of the magnificent fruit that grows somewhere in her town, perhaps within walking distance of the First Settler. The young waitress could easily walk out to the farm and bring back an apronfull by lunchtime. "My dad raises tomatoes," the woman muses as she hands me my change. "They just keep coming on, and I guess we could bring some of them to the restaurant."

Driving back to Pittsburgh, no longer hungry but my appetite unappeased, I anticipate dinner with Kathleen. One good meal will make up for a poor one. This hope keeps us going from table to table, seeking the perfect meal—or even the perfect tomato. Kathleen waits for me in Pittsburgh, and later, the results of my second PSA will indicate that my score has dropped down into a safe area. No further probing is necessary, my doctor will say. But, it is only a reprieve, of course, and my journey continues north on Route 7 back through Fly and then East Liverpool. Damn death and damn all those that threaten death. I look forward to the next meal. And the next. And the next.

Montaigne's
Bordeaux

Bordeaux has been known for its wines since the Romans introduced viticulture to this southwestern region of their province of Gaul. But this crescent-shaped city on the west bank of the Garonne River is also noted for Michel de Montaigne, the inventor of the personal essay who served as a jurist and a two-term mayor of Bordeaux in the sixteenth century.

His family name was Eyquem, but we know him by the appellation taken from the hill town of Montaigne, some thirty miles east of Bordeaux where his family's estate was situated. There he managed vineyards, made wine, and wrote his essays. But, fine horseman that he was, the city was still too far for him to effectively perform his mayoral duties, so he took up residence around 1581 in a house on a corner of what is now rue de la Rouselle.

Number 25 de la rue Rouselle is a typical stone house of the period, with a tall ground floor and upper rooms with low ceilings. The narrow, winding street is just two blocks from the busy port that is today mostly occupied by cruise ships. In the sixteenth century the docks were piled with cargoes of wine, dye stuff, and salted fish and meats that were loaded onto sturdy ships for the trip downriver to the Atlantic some sixteen miles away. The Garonne joins the Dordogne River to form the Gironne, which then serenely glides by vineyards whose names are familiar among the potable greats: Margaux, Medoc, Pauillac, Lafitte Rothschild to name a few.

Montaigne's old neighborhood today is probably quieter than when it was a place of commerce and trade that housed dealers of every material and produce, including wine. The essayist preferred the country routines of his manor, and of course the stone tower where he thought he was retiring in 1571, at the age of thirty-eight, to almost casually invent a new art form that has influenced writers ever since. What he would think of the contemporary term "creative nonfiction" is something to ponder, because he never put a name to his creation, referring to them as *essais*, or attempts, which incidentally gave name to the new form. In his own time they were read and translated—he was an overnight sensation—and imitated. The ideas advanced in several clearly prompted that keenest of cullers, William Shakespeare, in his plays *The Tempest*, *All's Well that Ends Well*, and even *King Lear* some scholars believe.

But in 1581 his solitary meditations were interrupted by his appointment as mayor of Bordeaux by the city's councilors at the behest of Henry III and the all-powerful Queen Mother, Catherine de Medici. It was an appointment Montaigne could scarcely refuse. This happened during the bloody period of the religious wars when Protestants and Catholics seemed to be barbecuing each other on every other street corner. Montaigne had the trust of both the Catholic Henry III and the Protestant Henry of Navarre. In fact, Navarre visited him at his estate on two occasions. The writer-made-politician shuttled between the opposing courts carrying proposals and information, so it seemed wise to name him, a devout Catholic, as mayor of a city that leaned toward the cause of Martin Luther. Moreover, the tenor of his essays just being published and admired marked him as a man of balanced judgment and equable sensitivity.

Montaigne may have looked upon the post as a fortuitous circumstance, for his essays had just begun to be made into books by Simon Millanges, a printer of Bordeaux. Millanges was also knowledgeable of both Latin and Greek which aided Montaigne, who had Latin but no Greek, in his quotations from the ancients. Another bonus, according to his own reports, was that the printer's shop was only "a short walk" from his house on rue de la Rouselle, and he could easily read proof and make the copious revisions in the margins of the large sheets being cranked out on the Millanges press while going about his mayoral duties.

The letterpress with moveable type was only about 150 years old at this time, and the effect of this astonishing technology was still shaking the Renaissance world. "I don't make the books," Montaigne observed, "the books make me." Apparently, the printer Millanges lived at No. 28 rue St. James, a few blocks south of rue Rouselle and adjoining the Crosse Cloche, one of the city's old medieval gates and very much a part of its skyline in Montaigne's day. Its huge bells ring out the start of the grape harvest, but its clocks were added in 1592, the year of Montaigne's death.

However, going north from his house for the same "short walk," is a one-block, narrow street named rue Millanges, and, as a novelist, I conjecture that the printer lived in one place but may have kept the cumbersome press and its heavy drawers of fonts at another location. Place Jullian adjoins rue Millanges and offers the motoring tourist a convenient parking garage in the "old town" beneath an open square with cafés and shops. Twenty such parking areas are maintained by the modern city to make its exploration an easy venture by car.

But on foot, and walking either way, Montaigne would not have had to face the Grand Prix traffic on the Cours Alsace de Lorraine or on the Cours Victor Hugo on his way to read proofs of the second edition of the *essais* in 1582. Today, these busy boulevards seem to pump animation into the modern city. It took me twelve minutes to walk from No. 25 rue de la Rouselle to the rue de Millanges where I am guessing the printer's shop was located. The morning sun would be over the essayist-mayor's right shoulder, and the sounds of the harbor accompanied his route as he mulled a digression on a chapter that Millanges was setting into type—say, "How We Cry and Laugh for the Same Thing." He would pass the Porte Callhau, the several-storied arch built in 1494 on the site of the city's former eastern gate. Today it houses interesting reconstructions of the city's history. A short distance further, he might have passed the Romanesque façade of St. Pierre, a twelfth century church that now fronts a charming square with cafés and shops.

Here I took lunch at the Terrasse Saint Pierre, a welcoming and cheerful restaurant with tables outside in good weather. It was after one o'clock in the afternoon and much too late for Montaigne who preferred his *dejeuner* at eleven. But the fare was delicious, and he would have cleaned up his plate with his fingers. He regarded the newfangled fork with disdain, thinking it was an unnecessary intervention between a man and his food. However, I used the utensil on an avocado stuffed with tiny prawns and a perfectly done salmon trout. A half bottle of a local rosé and some cheese in lieu of dessert brought the bill to about one hundred francs or around twelve dollars at the current rate of exchange, *service compris.*

Then on to Millanges's shop. No copyright provisions protected an author's work then, and it was the printers-turned-publishers—like Simon Millanges—who held licenses from the royal court to produce their books. These warrants somewhat protected the authors, too, given their relationship with their printers. It also gave the king and his government control over what Gutenberg's remarkable invention was putting into the public cognizance.

Montaigne apparently had a good relationship with Millanges and all of his subsequent publishers. He also supplied the paper for his books; not an uncommon arrangement, and Montaigne's particular sheets of paper bore the watermark of a heart.

The magnificent St. Andrea Cathedral, along with its separate Pey-Berlan bell tower, was also a part of the city's sixteenth-century skyline, but today's visitor has many more sites to admire and visit. First among these is the Centre Jean Moulin, a collection and memorial to the life and heroism of the French Resistance figure who was murdered here by the Nazi Gestapo during World War II. Only a short walk north from this museum is the Musée d'Aquitaine on the Cours Pasteur where the remains of Montaigne rest in an ornate marble sarcophagus as part of this museum's outstanding anthropological collection.

The hamlet of Montaigne where he died is only an hour's easy drive east of Bordeaux. On the way, one might lunch or pause in the small town of Castillon-la-Bataille where, as the name suggests, a conflict took place. This battle ended the English rule of France. Because of Eleanor of Aquitaine's marriage into the Plantagenet family, the English took over this huge part of France while drinking its wine and even naming some of it—claret. But that occupation came to an end, along with its attending Hundred Years War, when the Brothers Bureau lined up their artillery in Castillon and literally blew the English off the field and out of France. It was the first such usage of heavy guns in warfare.

This side trip to the town of Montaigne must be made on a Tuesday or Wednesday, for Montaigne's famous tower is only open to the public on those days, and sometimes that schedule is not always observed. But it is worth the effort to climb to the third floor of this corner tower of the manor house and to walk within its rounded area where the discursive shape of the personal essay came to light. With the exception of his large library, long ago dispersed to other archives, the room is much as he describes it in his essay "On Three Kinds of Relationships." The original manor house was destroyed by fire in the mid-nineteenth century and then rebuilt, but the tower and the stone steps he climbed to this top-floor study are the same. Incidentally, from here he could also heed the activity of his farm. The winepress was just across the courtyard.

His heart is buried in the small Romanesque church in the village, interred with his father in the same grave behind the modest altar. Francoise Eyquem de Montaigne took the rest of her husband to Bordeaux to be buried in the Church of the Feuillants even though the rectors of St. Andrea offered space in the cathedral. However, the archbishop apparently overruled their invitation, uneasy about some of Montaigne's skeptical musings about men and women and society—especially as expressed in "Apology for Raymond Sebond," in which he questioned the accepted views of human power and place in the universe.

A few years later, renovations saw his remains moved to different locations, and thence unfolded a near farcical play of movable tombs. Come the French Revolution, the New Citizens reasoned that he was too much of a philosopher to be buried in a church—an ironic seconding of the archbishop's thinking three centuries before—so he was moved to the then-newly established Bordeaux Society of Sciences, Letters, and Arts. Or so they thought. Apparently, it was the remains of a niece by marriage that had been so enshrined in 1800. Eighty years later, the original tomb was discovered and opened and its holdings recasketed and stored in a depository for several more years. At last, in 1886—almost five hundred years after his death—his ashes were placed in a marble sarcophagus, and this tomb was placed at the entrance to the Faculties of Theology, Science, and Letters of the University of Bordeaux. This building has since become the Musée d'Aquitaine, and the former mayor of Bordeaux lies in state in the first exhibit room on the ground floor.

The recumbent figure lies in full armor, helm and gloves beside him, so it comes as a shock to remember that this ultimate man of letters also served his king on horseback and in battle. However, it is the same neat, well shaped head represented in the painting by Thomas de Leu and a closer inspection gives up, I think, the familiar sly, skeptical cast around the eyes that indicates a detour is about to be made from the narrative. But the light was dim.

The Bordelaise enjoy food, wine, and talk as much as they did in his day. Montaigne loved to talk, loudly and in tumbling phrases according to his own self-portrait. "The Art of Discussion" was one of Pascal's favorite essays. But we drink the wine differently, store and revere the age of a vintage, while the wine from the essayist's vineyard, and those of his peers, was drunk fresh and within the year of its making. And tastes in food have markedly changed as well, for Mexican fare seems to be very popular now, and many restaurants of this cuisine are doing well in the modern city. However, the city's tables are yet resplendent with *fruits des mer* as they were in his time.

I tried to follow my guidebook's recommendation of Chez Phillipe on Parliament Square, but it was a Monday evening and this restaurant was closed. But just next door was Fernand Bistro Marin where I took a table outside and enjoyed oysters and a small whole bass grilled with fennel that could not have been better. A chilled bottle of Les Croix Blaches, a dry white Bordeaux of '95 vintage, was a perfect accompaniment. From my table I could admire the passing citizenry of Bordeaux also choosing their dinners from the menus posted by the different restaurants around this large, handsome plaza with Louis XV façades. This area was a royal market in Montaigne's day, and it was easy for me to imagine, no doubt my fancy made easier by the complex piquancy of the Croix Blanches, the essayist stepping across this square to inspect some legumes. Millanges's shop was just a few blocks away, and the essayist may have just come from adding a few sentences to "On Cannibals." Or perhaps, as mayor he had managed to soothe the feelings of upriver vintners not allowed to market their wines until December. Or perhaps he chose a post-*dejeuner* snack. Perhaps a peach. I settled for the usual crème brûlée.

Loitering on
the Loire

We must wear our distinctions within ourselves . . .

Has a ring to it—something Montaigne might have tossed off before inspecting his vineyards, but the phrase appears in one of my journals, sandwiched within notes made during a tour of the Loire Valley. I have been ambling westward of Orléans on N152 and have stopped for the night in Meung, at the Hotel St. Jacques, one of two hotels in this village of six thousand.

. . . those ornaments and emblems of rank given us by others or with which fate has blessed us.

On this afternoon, I am welcomed to the St. Jacques by an enthusiastic young couple I assume to be the new owners of this modest hostelry. She's in charge of the front, does the accounts, and he does the cooking. No doubt they plan renovations, for the hotel has seen better days. The large courtyard in the rear where I have parked my rented Citroen still has horse stalls, and the shower in my room resembles a large accordion.

If honors have worth, their value will show in our actions and our words, making it unnecessary to fix the signs of their recognition on our sleeves.

Are these my words? Do I really talk like this in unguarded moments? There's an Augustan stamp on the rhetoric, a lordly

217

loft to the musing that I can't identify as mine; yet, the lines are scribbled here in my journal within the usual tourist sighting and the flavorful remembrance of the meal I had the previous night in Gien, where the chef-owner of the Poularde is a master of *foie gras avec comporte des poires*. Yet, I see myself penning these lines as I sit in the threadbare lounge of the St. Jacques, sipping a pastis before dinner. The young woman who welcomed me earlier has brought me the aperitif, for she turns out not to be the owner but one of several waitresses who are now setting up the tables in the dining room.

The actual *patron* reigns within a tidy bar of etched mirrors and cut glass. The crystal festoons of a chandelier overhead do not lighten her sour expression, and she seems to be reckoning the cost of cleaning their smudged facets. Yet it is a cozy nook. The rattle and occasional blare of traffic on the rue DeGaulle on the other side of the curtained front windows creates a smug satisfaction within me. I am at rest on the plush velvet divan while other travelers are still on the road, and to savor the anise of the pastis is to amplify that distinction. Possibly, it also oils the imperious tone of my introspection.

For its size, Meung embraces a very large history. It was here that Jean de Meung was born and later, in 1280, penned the final eighteen thousand lines of his classic *Romance of the Rose*, one of those great books that no one reads anymore, though I remember my mother trying to interest me in it. The medieval poet wrote in a period, my Michelin wryly comments, that "did not lack readers of stamina."

François Villon was the only prisoner not to perish in the local chateau's dungeon, having been freed by Louis XI. Not so lucky, the Duke of Salisbury died in the same chateau from wounds he suffered in the siege of Orléans, a few kilometers east of Meung. That siege was eventually lifted by Joan of Arc in 1429, and as part of her strategy, she recaptured from the English the bridge here at Meung that spans the Loire.

Not the present bridge of course, which I inspected earlier as these pretentious axioms for modest behavior were gathering force in my mind. I can see myself putting down this plea for decorum within the mill of celebrity—a status for which I cannot speak but, in all probability, hope for—as I pour more water into the pastis. But I am unable to freshen the cause of this moral rant. I have traveled only eighty-three kilometers this day from Gien, and my notes reveal no significant detour that could have inspired the decree. In Orléans I had paused to pay the obligatory visit to the cathedral and the enormous promenade around it, spending only an hour or two at this landmark of French history where a young woman's heroic zeal turned back the English invader and saved her country from ignominy. Where, by the way, did the Maid of Orléans wear her honors?

These self-made pilgrimages I make on the back roads of France are meant to idle my mind and pave the rifts in my patchwork career as a writer-academic. The pageantry of the French countryside is meant to soothe my common anxieties, and the reasonable rows of a vineyard or the savory of a newly mowed field are supposed to sedate my ordinary concerns. The trill of blackbirds on the roadside is an innocent distraction.

But my happy numbness this day must have been nicked by a discordant thought. I review the journal's pages. Yes, dinner at the Poularde the night before already noted; nothing in that. I had stayed there once before and returned to sample the foie gras again, followed by *rognons de veau* and with a half bottle of a white Sancerre. My notes say the wine was "smooth."

Some lines testify to the loneliness encountered on these jaunts, a kind of self-willed punishment for leaving Kathleen even for just a week. But I enjoy these bouts of melancholy. "Do we create out of loneliness," I write on this first day in the Loire. "Solitude settles within us like a grain of sand around which we lacquer layers of imagery—putting a gloss on our apartness; giving it a bright finish for the world to reflect upon." Lacquer layers, indeed—something in that Sancerre perhaps.

In the same paragraph, I reflect upon my children. I have come upon one of those crossroads where one looks each way, sums up progress made thus far. One daughter is inexplicably estranged, another faces career challenges, and my son yet seeks his own rhythm, his own path. He has been a chef, and I may have projected his image upon the young couple who greeted me at the St. Jacques earlier, for I sometimes fantasize him happily mated and established. So the young couple disappoint me when I discover them to be only part of the hotel's staff—not the owners. I must work toward tolerance, patience. Maybe they are not really interested in serving people like me as a life's work—it's only a summer job.

After setting down the aperitif and a small pitcher of water, the young woman has joined the other waitresses preparing the dozen tables in the next room. Her partner—and are they even together?—passes back and forth through the swinging door into the kitchen. He wears a white smock with a napkin knotted around his neck, and it is evident he is following orders from inside the kitchen. Maybe the chef is the old guy who showed me where to park in the back courtyard earlier, his suspenders flapping around his behind and his creased face whitely stubbled. I had thought he was a handyman I had roused from his afternoon nap.

Perhaps in these journal pages I am wagging a cautionary finger at myself for attempting to wear my children as ornaments on my sleeve. Pride in an offspring's accomplishments—as well as the converse disappointment—is but a superficial emblem of the relationship, a self-serving display, whereas the genuine value of the bond is measured by allegiance and affection—in the fealty of the love within the embrace, however awkward. No citations are required.

It is only about 7:30 p.m., so I have the dining room to myself. Even in Meung people dine late. The waitresses move among the tables adjusting glassware, checking the correctness of a setting. Two stand by the sideboard and chat. They have been costumed in black skirts and white blouses with dainty white aprons tied around their waists. The ensemble is a quaint souvenir of bygone times no doubt sustained by Madame Patron. The St. Jacques has its own standards. A waitress has just brought me a basket of bread. I assume these are local girls working to supplement a family income; some may be putting money aside for marriage and others for a new life in Paris. Madame has trained them well for they are casually expert in their performance in the dining room, and the dignity with which they do their work honors the house.

Poets donning working class personae is scribbled after my call for modest behavior. The vanity of certain writers must have been on my mind, must have slipped through the screen of black-birds' song. Currently, a kind of romance with the working class has been refigured in rock stars and fashions—the blue collar is in—and some poets have joined the union as well, others have advanced the cause. One I know even wears bib overalls, thick work shoes, and a crisp miner's cap. The labor of lifting a poetry workshop is heavy work indeed. This man's poems are sentimental grievances, a dreary array of complaints on behalf of people he only vaguely knows and far from the candid pathos immortalized by Eugene Smith or Walker Evans.

There's been a discussion about dessert. The St. Jacques keeps a traditional table so the whole meal, from soup to nuts as we used to say in Kansas City—though I don't remember ever getting any nuts in Kansas City—is all determined from the beginning. My notes say I have "refused" dessert, but maybe I only declined to choose this final course before I have eaten the meal. At the S&W Cafeteria in Kansas City, we never went back for the pie until we had mopped up the last of the gravy on the Salisbury steak. The same young woman who had served me the pastis is also my waitress—a graceful and pleasant continuity. She describes each dish almost as if she might be preparing it at table. One word has evaded my hesitant hearing of the language. It sounds as if she is saying, "navy."

Yes, she nods.

"Navy?" I ask again.

With an innocent aggression, she picks up the notebook and pen beside my plate that I have been using and carefully prints the word in the middle of my call for humility. N-A-V-E-T. Of course—turnip—even Julia Child recommends the vegetable, so I order the lamb stew. My ignorance, exposed by this exchange, is overlooked by the waitress as she rejoins her colleagues with a polite indifference.

But this morning in Pittsburgh, as I turn the pages of my journal and come to her plain block letters, the *N* of *navet*, made just so, calls up the whole ambiance of that evening at the St. Jacques. The bleak lighting of the room, an illumination the French seem to favor in restaurants; the crisp feel of the table linen; and the flaky deliciousness of the bread in my mouth—all are summoned by this young tutor's handwriting in my notebook. No record of the wine that accompanied the meal; something red and maybe a Bourgueil.

But I have been unfair to single out poets, as it is always unfair to single out poets. They are only reflecting the strut and gab of the culture that has borne them. Pride, Ben Franklin is supposed to have observed, was the ruling passion of his new America, and I don't think the fever has broken. Our leaders swagger into adventures, unprepared for the aftermath of their hubris, as they have ignored its immorality. We have become accessories to their vanity and too many of us celebrate their conceit. Has self-importance ever been so honored and so decorated?

What's for dessert? My notes make no mention of a choice, perhaps I skipped it. The *navarin* has been completely satisfying, the silky texture to its sauce comes from the lowly turnip. My waitress has become somewhat formal; the meal done, the intimacy of our casual association has been folded up and laid aside. We correct our appearances if not our differences. Tomorrow is Easter Sunday and Chinon lies ahead where the red wine is said to be an "ethereal shadow of the Medoc."

Proud Flesh

We were a congenial bunch in the 1960s, restoring old farm-houses in the Livingston domain of Duchess and Columbia counties in New York State and doing a lot of drinking and dining in those farmhouses, where the women were all handsome and marvelous cooks, and the men were writers and artists—left-leaning and rather smug. Joe McCarthy had been destroyed and the insipid placidity of the Eisenhower years was behind us. We had welcomed and grieved for the Kennedys and swaggered like the manqué Marxists we were with the self-flattering panache of James Bond.

The distinguished journalist Richard Rovere and his wife, Eleanor, lived in Rhinebeck. The noted book illustrators Martin and Alice Provensen were in Clinton Corners. Mary Lee Settle lived near Barrytown, I think. Gore Vidal lived in Tivoli in a house that John Jay Chapman had built for his wife right on the edge of the Hudson River. In fact, it was called Edgewater. Chanler Chapman, the essayist's son, ran a dairy farm nearby and, with his wife Helen, played at being a kooky patron and served, unknowingly or not, as the model for the title character in Saul Bellow's *Henderson the Rain King*. Bellow had lived in an apartment on the Chapman estate when he taught at Bard College near Red Hook.

The dinner parties were fabulous and fun—brilliant talk, gossip, and jokes passed with the cassoulet and the flan. Wine and whiskey flowed freely. Often F. W. Dupee of the *Partisan Review* would be encountered standing near a carved mantel, soberly assessing the party if not the chances of the republic surviving. On the day Hemingway shot himself, Gore Vidal popped into an afternoon cocktail gathering to announce, "Everyone moves up one!" On another evening, in a sort of parlor game, we contributed one-liners to Rovere's upcoming spoof, "The American Establishment," that was to be published by the *American Scholar* and that was to confound and even alarm certain world leaders. "What's this I read about an unelected establishment that runs your country?" Nehru was supposed to have asked Jack Kennedy upon his arrival for a state visit.

But with all our drinking and foolery, we were also dedicated to our typewriters and to our different employments of language and image. The hardest worker of us all might have been William Humphrey.

He and Dorothy had redone a farmhouse set in an orchard near the village of Claverack, just outside of Hudson. They had moved onto its wide-planked floors gorgeous, genuine pieces of Empire furniture that were not always so comfortable to sit on. They had not always lived so well—these furnishings and the house itself were a result of the success of his first novel, *Home from the Hill*, published in 1957. A movie had been made of the book, and there were many subsequent publications and foreign translations. Only a few years before, they had scrimped by as managers of a goat farm and lived in an apartment over a garage—part of their compensation. Theodore Weiss, an early champion of Bill's work, brought him to Bard College to teach.

The poet also introduced us just as my own first novel, *The Common Pasture*, was published in 1967. His second novel, *The*

Ordways, had appeared three years earlier. Bill Humphrey was a small, neatly made man with an East Texan twang to his voice that he could artfully modulate to suit a mordant account of his boyhood in Texas or an acerbic judgment of a contemporary. "He doesn't have the legs for it," he would say, the narrow-set eyes twinkling as the long, thin nose seemed to spear the opinion in midair. The briar pipe in his mouth was elegantly turned, and the tobacco smoldering in its bowl was mailed to him every month, a pound at a time, from a tobacconist in St. Louis. I smoked a pipe then also and immediately put my name on the mailing list. Heywood Mixture.

What I'm saying is that his vanity was no more mortal than what afflicted any of us, it was just that he seemed to take more pleasure in it or that his impoverished childhood gave him license to splurge his hard-earned success a little. He did not put on clothes so much as he donned apparel, and the sport jackets and trim slacks looked to be from F. R. Tripler rather than Brooks or J. Press. He passed on to me, in a confidence that completely turned my head, the name of a "decent tailor" on Saville Row as well as the location of "a rather splendid cobbler in Firenze." He served the best of Bordeaux and always suggested to Dorothy that we take dessert in one of the formal parlors at the front of the house. But with all that, he was dedicated to his craft and art.

"You're from good people," he said to my first wife, Polly, one evening, and he meant from the good part of town, from the affluent side of the railroad tracks. His memoir *Far from Heaven* (1977) enhanced this poor-boy image, though there was occasional talk that his family did have money. It might be remembered that many of his protagonists, starting with the first novel, all wear a bar sinister that keeps them from the rich pickings of the main table. He claimed to have American Indian blood in his veins, Cherokee if I remember, as a further proof of his estrangement.

This romantic side of him was also embellished by his pursuit of game in both field and stream. Hemingway had taught him to hunt and fish—he claimed, from a close reading of the master's work—and he put this knowledge, either first or secondhand, into the graceful narrative of his small masterpiece *The Spawning Run* (1970), a sly account of salmon fishing in Scotland.

One day he called to ask if he could come down to our old farm to hunt some birds. He parked the small vw station wagon below our house and stepped forth as if from the pages of an Abercrombie and Fitch catalog. His costume looked freshly pressed, a sporty tweed cap cocked on his head, and puttees expertly fixed around his calves. The bird dog belonged in an ad for expensive bourbon. The shotgun that hung casually in the crook of his arm had been handmade for him in England he informed me before he walked off into the scrub of our bottom field. Only about an hour later, I looked out the window to find his car gone—our grounds were poor in game, he said later.

My wife had begun to become impatient with Bill's chronic name dropping, his dust bowl snobbery. But in my admiration and affection, I overlooked these habits, because wonderful stories—wonderfully told stories—would often result. His reports of dinners with his publishers, Alfred and Blanch Knopf—and in their home in Chappaqua no less—provided close-up views of this legendary couple. An interview on a French radio program, of course implying his fluency with the language, also recalled an off-color remark by Sartre that, alas, could not be effectively translated into English. Katherine Anne Porter was a mentor and friend who entertained the Humphreys in Charlottesville. She even had Bill chauffeured into Washington in the limousine provided her by the University of Virginia so he could join a Vietnam War protest and march on the Nixon White House. He told us with a twangy blandness that he had marched with a contingent of homosexual businessmen. The limousine picked him up at day's end and returned him to Miss Porter's table for dinner. The next week, he was on the phone to ask me to join him in a similar protest rally in the city of Hudson, and we walked together.

In 1969 my second novel, *An American Marriage*, was published, and I felt it was a breakthrough book for me—I sensed I had made purchase on the strands of character and place that must weave into a novel. Macmillan quickly put the book into a second edition, the Book of the Month Club offered it to its subscribers, and a movie deal was signed. With all of our back-and-forth in each other's houses, I had never felt the friendship was balanced, but now I felt more comfortable with him. "Yes," he said, tapping down his pipe and relighting it, "it's a harmless book."

Proud Flesh, his third novel, was published in 1973. Christopher Lehmann-Haupt reviewed it in the daily edition of the *New York Times* of April 4, and his response is probably the most viciously constructed condemnation of a writer's work in modern history. For starters, he says the novel is "the worst piece of fiction I've read so far this year," and that it is an "awfulness." To further unsheathe his wit, he writes that even "the title stinks a little." Lehmann-Haupt levels "balderdash" at Humphrey's prose while crediting him with "an inexhaustible stockpile of clichés. . . . Do I make it sound awful?" the reviewer pauses to take a vituperative breath. "It gets worse."

Phones began to ring in the mid-Hudson Valley. We were stunned and staggered by the violence of this attack on one of our own. Yet, I wonder now how many of us were not also a little pleasured by the savagery and were secretly gleeful that the book reviewer had evened the score, for some of us, for Bill's occasional hauteur, his self-made and self-taught criteria that few of us could meet. Perhaps a sort of telepathy transmitted these feelings because the letters expressing outrage and sympathy were never answered and Dorothy coolly fended off phone calls. With the exception of Ted and Renee Weiss, who had moved to Princeton, and another couple who were never a part of the group, no one was to hear from Bill Humphrey again. He had posted "No Trespassing" signs around that elegantly furnished house in the apple orchard.

Well, that's not entirely true.

In 1992 St. Martin's published my second collection of short stories, *Success*, which included a story entitled "The Catch." The protagonist of this story, originally appearing in the *North American Review*, refers to *The Spawning Run* and identifies its author. My phone rang one morning, and into my ear came the dry twang of Bill Humphrey's voice—the twenty years that separated our last talk disappeared with the first sounds. He called to thank me for mentioning him and his book in my story. The good, good office of Ted Weiss was responsible for his knowing of it. Bill and I chatted easily; we could have been finishing some topic started at dinner only the night before, but much had happened in the meantime. Governments and leaders had come and gone. Our group had been dispersed by death and destiny. Polly and I had divorced, and I now lived in Pittsburgh. Bill still lived in Columbia County in the farmhouse, but Dorothy was living with her daughter from an earlier marriage. He was alone and feeling poorly. In fact, he was dying and, I was to learn later, being cared for by a hospice team. He died in 1997.

Those of us who endeavor to trace a small segment of our place and time into words and then limn these onto paper are conscious sometimes of our audacity, our hubris. It is a little thing we do and it may seem to grow in importance in the solitude of our keep. "The work is all," our godfather Henry said. Yes, it is all, and it is also nothing.

Unwired

This guy rings our doorbell and offers me one hundred dollars for one of the insulators that sit like glass bells on the top sills of our front windows. He wants the blue one, what I would call a Chagall blue, with the "No. 19" embossed on its skirt along with the name of its maker—the Hemingray Company. The same company also made the other ones, and our assortment caught his collector's eye as he passed by on the street.

A couple of them are of clear glass, two more in shades of blue, and another one is amber. They seem to be made of poured glass, and their acorn shape is ringed by ridges and grooves designed to separate and hold the different transmission lines that once pulled across their glass surfaces. I don't remember how we came by them; most likely they were found objects in this old house we have restored, but they still conduct energy of a different sort: a refracted light that ornaments the front room to ignite the eye and signal the senses.

As a boy I spied insulators like these on the cross-arms of utility poles that stood sentry along the route of visits to relatives in Kansas. From the backseat of my grandfather's Buick they appeared to be currants or raisins my grandmother may have forgot to put into the breakfast muffins, for they had become black against the prairie sky. Their different colors could not be appreciated from the ground. Sometimes a crow or a few meadowlarks would land to perch between them and make their dressed file irregular and perhaps lend a different pulse to the humming lines.

Their various colors described the kind of lines that they suspended above and across the country—whether power lines or telephone cables—and I would guess these colors were coded to tell linemen what sort of voltages they repaired and carefully lifted into place. Some carried electricity and others carried the homely language of family history. "Mother died this morning. Come home."

But that wasn't always the case. Originally these different hues of blue and amber, the clear glass, were irrelevant to their usage. The same companies that made the glass jars that mid-nineteenth-century homemakers used to put up fruit and vegetables for winter meals were enlisted to make insulators for Mr. Morse's crackling telegraph lines. Initially these wires were buried underground, but their messages became short-circuited and diminished by leakage, so it was reasoned to lift them overhead and on poles. But as any of us who went to Scarritt School could have told them, the wooden poles would draw the messages into the ground with the same corruption. So some kind of object had to be found that would come between the wood, the current, and the messages carried on the wire. Ceramic doorknobs were first used but they were impractical, for the wires would easily slip off their smooth roundness and short out. Then, someone invented this glass acorn with ridges that held the wires in place, and a whole industry was created—out of scrap.

The glass left over from the primary product—canning jars— was remelted and poured into the molds so they could be of any color. If the Hemingray Company had made their famous Globe jars in azure in the morning, then azure insulators would be turned out in the afternoon If clear glass had been used for fruit jars, then the insulators next produced would be clear. And so on. It was one of those fortuitous happenstances of human endeavor that no longer seems possible. Today, the waste of our ingenuity must be buried out of sight almost guiltily and is useless.

The color of the different insulators became relevant when electrical lines joined those that carried telegraph messages and, later, the human voice, and it became important to tell one line from another on the poles that began to staple the countryside. The insulators themselves became more sophisticated. A hollow space about the size of a broomstick is cast within each and threaded so that the unit can be screwed down over a corresponding thread in the wooden peg fixed on the pole's cross-arm. The first insulators had no such design and were merely fitted down over a smooth peg, but experience showed that a storm could blow them off their perch to interrupt the transmission. The Hemingray Company also added their own innovation, duly patented, of a serrated edge around the bottom of the insulators, and these little points were meant to drain rain water quickly and therefore minimize the interference caused by a natural phenomenon—always a threat to human invention.

I knew of such challenges firsthand because of my Saturday afternoons spent at the Chief Theatre where Jimmy Cagney and Pat O'Brien would regularly meet disasters with heroic insouciance. In one film they were fast-talking linemen, vying for the gentle goodness of a Wendy Barrie, but then the lines go down. "It's the tower on Brown's Ridge," O'Brien shouts through the onslaught. Water runs in rivulets from the hood of his lineman's slicker.

"I'll hook it up," Cagney says with that lopsided grin that lets you know that he knows he will die in the process. But kindly Dr. Christian, remarkably au courant with the latest info from the Mayo brothers, had been about to save Wendy Barrie's little sister when the lights went out. But Cagney lifts the right cable back onto the No. 19 blue insulator made by the Hemingray Company—someday to be collected and worth a hundred dollars—and the lights go back on. At the same time a pip, like the flare of a match, occurs at the top of the tower on Brown's Ridge.

Such melodramas are quaint and amusing today when put beside the internal storms of personality that absorb us: the mannered cruelties between children and parents, the psychic wounds we have been educated to look for as we dress for the day. All of it energy gone awry. Moreover, the new modes of communication, handheld and wireless, require no insulators from the Hemingray Company; in fact they stopped making them in 1967. So what is to protect us standing on the ground from this promiscuous energy and raw immediacy? No longer confined to cables, our humdrumming pollutes waiting rooms and restaurants and even innocent street corners. We are swamped by our own accessibility and even threatened on the highway by this wanton facility as some state legislatures have recently determined.

"I don't want to know all this," my grandmother often complained in response to some report in the *Kansas City Star* of an overnight brutality. What she meant was, did she need to know this information to keep house for my grandfather, pack my school lunch, change the bed linen, and bread the fish for supper? But the item became an inert particle within her soft sensibility, and today the continual fallout of the commonplace buries us—our bins overflow. Plains storms no longer threaten the hookup because the current onslaught is self-generated trivia, and nothing can insulate us from the force of its insignificance. It is an irony, foreign to those old movies, that the genius of our recent inventions has only exposed how really boring and paltry we are.

Maybe we have reached that stage in our history on Earth when we have nothing more to say that is interesting, that after a few million years or so, it's all been talked out. The limitations on travel to other worlds have become discouragingly obvious, and perhaps we are similarly bound to subject matter. The trajectory of our chatter follows the Earth's curvature; our words do not fly up so much as they go round and round and round—faster but the same words.

In the horror of the last century, the risks of intelligence have so shocked us that we reach for the banal, and not just with a cell phone but in our politics, our literature—our quotidian. Jimmy Cagney is dead, and no one seems willing to handle fresh ideas. A residual meditation plays in the depth of this azure glass on my windowsill, and I have just learned its value.

The End of Something

An obituary in the morning paper gives the short biography of a scientist whose inventive genius enabled explorations of the ocean floor several miles down. Reading of his life, I share historical moments with him.

When he attended high school in New Jersey, Mussolini and Hitler came to power, Amelia Earhart disappeared, and our dog Sucre was stolen from our front yard in Kansas City. The obit also says he was studying aeronautical engineering at UCLA when FDR died and as Hemingway moved to Cuba to begin writing *The Old Man and the Sea*. I have left Kansas City by then to finish high school in New Hampshire, where I learned to ski and lost my virginity.

So, these two histories are joined to become one, and as I sip a second cup of coffee, memory ties up my chronicle with his. One incident recalled pulls out another that in turn snags one more, so a skein of happenings, put aside in a lobe of my brain, has been exposed as in a messy pantry. A line of narrative can sometimes untangle them, order them, and—like the best jokes—these memories are related in the present tense.

I am fifteen and at school in Wolfeboro, New Hampshire, and it is 1944. I have volunteered to be a plane spotter as part of the nation's civil defense against the possibility of air raids by the German Luftwaffe. Village carpenters have erected a sturdy block-house in an open field near the school where volunteers monitor the sparse air traffic, reporting the occasional civilian or military aircraft via a telephone directly connected to headquarters in Portsmouth. This outpost is a snug two-storied construction with a wood-burning stove that keeps the interior ferociously hot in winter. Large panes of glass are fitted around all four sides of the second floor to provide unobstructed views of the fields outside, Lake Winnipesaukee nearby, and the foothills of the White Mountains in the distance. The phone is installed here at one end of the built-in settee that has been made comfy by a thick, tufted cushion that could have been designed, and probably was, for the cockpit of one of the large yachts that sometimes decorate the lake. It is here I do my homework as I wait to report the infrequent plane to civil defense headquarters. It is here I wait for Nancy.

From the vantage of my elevated shelter, I can see her approach at a great distance. As I say, it is winter, and she appears as a slim figure, walking resolutely toward my sentry post, hunched against the cold and her schoolbooks clamped under one arm. She is coming from her last class, on her way home, and brings assignments in trigonometry for us to ponder. She's better at it than I. How these particular study sessions began I cannot remember, and if I attempted to detail the course of their unfolding, the narrative would become chaotic. Nietzsche has cautioned that a life without forgetting is impossible, and it is a problem experienced by historians and storytellers alike—what to leave out and what to put in.

So I will simply greet Nancy at the door on the ground floor where we will embrace well below the glassed enclosure of the floor above—out of sight. She is stamping her feet as I warm her plump cheeks with my kisses. She can only stay for a little while because she must get home to fix supper for her younger brothers. Their mother is a nurse at the small clinic in town. Nancy climbs the ladder to the second floor, puts down her books, and kicks off her heavy boots. I sometimes rub her feet through the thick socks she wears as she tells me of some prank at school, something a teacher said, something that I have missed as I performed my duty spotting planes. We try a few trig problems but often duck down below the line of vision to kiss. She has pulled the heavy sweater she wears over her head, tousling her long black hair, just as a small plane alerts my attention. I call Portsmouth. As I describe the plane, its direction, and estimated altitude, Nancy carefully unbuttons her corduroy slacks and slips them off. She folds the trousers neatly and puts them exactly at one end of the settee, then perches on her knees to witness me doing my duty. Her face is sweet with an amused expectancy, and like the math problems, she knows more about what we are about to do than I.

From the ground level, what we are about to do cannot be seen—only the top half of our persons, appropriately clothed. Our visible animation can be attributed to teens chatting. Not many people come by the station anyway, only a local now and then walking down to the lake to check his ice-fishing rig. From the air, the pilot of a plane, suspicious or not, could easily identify our activity, but only if he flew at tree level—an unlikely possibility—and we giggle at the duality of our deception. At the same time, I keep an eye out over her shoulder for Nazi bombers. Later, we do more trigonometry and then once more demonstrate one of the discipline's six basic functions before Nancy gets dressed and heads home. I watch her trudge through the crusted snow as she gradually disappears into the azure of the late-afternoon light. That night at supper—I am one of a dozen of the school's boarders—we are served corn chowder and cheese biscuits, and I can taste their flavor and texture as I write these words.

So those flavors and Nancy's capricious gift of herself rise from the depths of memory to float on the surface of my reflections this morning, made buoyant by reading the history of someone who invented a device that explored the Titanic, another dream that sank into the subconscious.

If the brain is an Internet that connects us with the past, then to have too much memory could be a problem, to tend Nietzsche again. Our circuits would become overloaded as we yearn for a certain past, a way of life that has disappeared, and our engagement with present circumstances becomes qualified. Some authorities in the nineteenth century considered nostalgia to be a fatal disease, and this diagnosis may have some validity today. When our present world becomes increasingly uninhabitable, the impulse to fly into a past that appears more hospitable, in a sort of homing instinct, becomes attractive. The term describing this condition was invented by a doctor in the seventeenth century who combined the Greek term for returning home *nostos*, with the word *algia* suggesting a painful condition. Someone who lives in the past may not be in physical pain, but a government that chooses the past as a forum for resolving contemporary challenges can bring disaster upon its citizenry. A yearning for the good old days, edited of ugliness and strife, is a shallow refuge from current conflicts, though looking back may satisfy our human urge for continuity. Maybe our identity can be located in the tumble of history and some order can be imposed on the shifting inventory of events that is memory. Proust's petite Madeleine is actually a big goddamn cookie.

As recounted elsewhere, my mother, in her later years, would review and edit her own historical narrative, giving herself leading roles and reducing another's lines—even to changing the truth of a character—all to bolster her sense of herself. For her, the old days were made even better by her deft manipulation of memory in which, alas, she ultimately became lost.

But weren't some of those old days really good?

A friend writes me of the train travel we can remember, citing the luxury and comfort dramatized in a film about the famed Orient Express. The mechanics of transporting a person from one place to another are still operating about the same, but the comfort and indulgence once experienced on those journeys are no longer available, and terminals like Pennsylvania Station in New York, palaces erected for the common citizenry, have either been torn down or nailed over with wallboard. I made the trip back and forth across half of the United States many times, and I can remember the near noiseless security of a Pullman car, the smell of coffee from the diner, and the sight of a smart cadre of waiters standing ready to serve me, all of whom seemed to answer to the same names—George or Walter. But does memory reflect the shameful history of that nomination as it fondly recalls it?

On sleepless nights, I make that trip again when a freight train's heavy murmur rises in the darkness outside my widows, passing through Pittsburgh on the same roadbed I once traveled from Kansas City to New York. Eventually its rumble fades, pulling me into sleep as it takes its different goods, the night, and my memories of old days to a distant terminal. We have become concerned by a condition that leaves the victim shipwrecked on an isle of the present, and perhaps our affection for nostalgia has irked the patience of certain gods, so they punish us with boundless forgetfulness. We fail to inform our present with our past; it no longer measures our selves but has become a park for idle amusement. So in relationships and in politics—even in an occasional essay—we try to remember who we are.

In Hemingway's story "The End of Something"—written decades before *The Old Man and the Sea* and far superior—a couple view the foundations of an old lumber mill as they fish in a lake offshore. "It seems more like a castle," the young woman says, sounding similar to that other Hemingway girl who imagines that the dry barren hills of Spain resemble white elephants. Both women are attempting to save a love affair gone dead, to keep the presence of a relationship alive by their particular imaginations. It is a sad story; how the mind attempts to create another world when the vitality of this one fails.

One early evening that summer in Kansas City, we take the cooling air on the front porch, and a faint click-click of nails against the sidewalk's surface gradually alerts us. "If I didn't know better," my grandfather says from behind the afternoon paper, "I'd say that sounds like Sucre coming down the street." Sucre was a handsome German Airedale who had taken the blue ribbon at the dog show that was part of the American Royal stock exposition. His picture had been in the *Kansas City Star*, accompanied by my grandmother because of her prominence in Democratic Party politics. My grandfather had named the dog in honor of Antonio José Sucre, the South American revolutionary and chief aide to Simón Bolívar. His military leadership freed that continent from Spanish rule, and he was a prominent figure in my grandfather's personal pantheon. "It was that picture in the paper that done it," my grandfather opined at supper on more than one occasion. "Thanks to Eleanor Roosevelt here," his fork poked toward my grandmother, "the thieves saw his picture in the paper and where we lived and scooped him up to breed him." I get the idea, and my grandmother seemed embarrassed, her usual olive complexion darkened, but I think now her change in color was from anger held back.

And it *is* Sucre. He trots down Roberts Street, across the front lawn, up the terrace, and then the porch steps to calmly lie down next to my grandfather's rocking chair. The dog properly places his front paws before him and licks his chops a couple of times and then looks up the street as if to reckon the distance he has traveled. Miraculously, after a couple of years, he found his way home. He's had adventures, but he has remembered where he came from.

In the American Lives series

Phantom Limb
by Janet Sternburg

Yellowstone Autumn
A Season of Discovery in
a Wondrous Land
by W. D. Wetherell

To order or obtain more information on these or other University of Nebraska Press titles, visit www.nebraskapress.unl.edu.

Other Works by Hilary Masters

NOVELS
Elegy for Sam Emerson
Home Is the Exile
The Harlem Valley Trio:
  Strickland
  Cooper
  Clemmons
Palace of Strangers
An American Marriage
The Common Pasture
Manuscript for Murder
  (under the pseudonym P. J. Coyne)

MEMOIR
Last Stands: Notes from Memory

SHORT FICTION
"How the Indians Buried Their Dead"
"Success"
"Hammertown Tales"

ESSAYS
"In Rooms of Memory"
"Shadows on a Wall: Juan O'Gorman
  and the Mural in Pàtzcuaro"
"In Montaigne's Tower"